THE
CHRISTIAN
EMPLOYEE

THE CHRISTIAN EMPLOYEE

by Robert Mattox

Bridge Publishing, Inc.
South Plainfield, NJ

**Unless otherwise noted,
biblical quotations in this book
are taken from the King James Version.**

THE CHRISTIAN EMPLOYEE
Copyright © 1978 by Robert M. Mattox
All Rights Reserved
Printed in the United States of America
International Standard Book Number: 0-88270-263-7
Library of Congress Catalog Card Number: 77-20588
Published by Bridge Publishing, Inc.
South Plainfield, NJ

To my beloved wife, Anne
and to our children,
Mark and Melissa,
for the love, support and encouragement
given by them to me
in this endeavor

Table of
Contents

A Special Acknowledgment

Once, while completing an employment qualification form, I came upon the following instruction: "List the foreign languages spoken by you." I filled in the blank with "English." My boss is still chuckling over that. But in my case the answer is probably more true than false. Anyone who has ever read my "engineering" language knows that I am far more adept with numbers than I am with words.

It is to Vickie Chandler that I owe a special debt of gratitude for translating my "foreign language" into clear English. Vickie spent many hours of structuring, editing and typing to produce the final version of this manuscript. For her patience, fortitude and competence, a sincere "thank you."

* * * *

Other Acknowledgments

Acknowledgment is gratefully made to the many people who have allowed me to share part of their Christian experiences in this book. These experiences certainly enrich the material and demonstrate the validity of God's Word.

To Derrel Emmerson and Jack Zirkle, a special "thank you" for giving me the opportunity and encouragement to begin this work.

Introduction

The text is complete. The work is finished. The collection of papers and notes, drafts and redrafts have been discarded. And I am left with the task of writing an introduction.

An introduction *should*, I suppose, provide a brief synopsis of the content of a book. An introduction *should* state the author's purposes in writing a book in the first place. It *should* be written so as to generate interest in the minds of the readers.

But it has been my prayer, throughout the preparation of this manuscript, that the Holy Spirit has *already* "generated interest" and placed a desire in the heart of the reader to find God's solutions to the problems and conflicts faced by the Christian in his secular world of employment.

I do not want to "grab" the reader's interest with promises of instant success on the job. This work very simply describes God's activity in and purposes for secular employment.

In this book, I have presented seven principles, each built upon the previous one. The principles are simple, straightforward and, according to my limited understanding, are scripturally founded. This is not a how-to book. The principles are just that—*principles*, not techniques. I have not attempted to give the reader step-by-step solutions to any and every problem that arises in secular employment environment. The principles present God's truth on the subject and as such are foundational elements. The reader must add to the principles faith, love, determination, and the Lord's uniqueness and creativity to arrive at God's solution to *specific* problems. The importance of prayer and the guidance of the Holy Spirit in this regard cannot be overemphasized.

God's principles for any area of life do not produce results unless they are applied. As we have seen in the lives of the Pharisees, scriptural knowledge which is not lived is actually dangerous. As I have been privileged to present this material at conferences and seminars, I have stressed the importance of applying, even *testing*, the principles, preferably after each unit of study or chapter. The results ranged from excitement to astonishment as participants returned to their offices and put God's principles into action. It is to these many brothers and sisters in Christ who "tried" God and found Him faithful that I am indebted, for it was through their encouragement that the Lord first prompted me to share His truths concerning employment in book form.

There is nothing new in the idea that our jobs play an important part in God's plan for this age, but I believe the church has simply overlooked or underestimated the importance of secular employment in its quest to become more "spiritual." As we have sought to increase our spiritual maturity, we have created a dichotomy between the Christian's role in the spiritual world and his role in the secular world. Jesus desires that we be "whole," meaning *one* and *integrated*. It is my hope that the latter portion of this book will aid us in restoring the "oneness" of our lives and thus our message to the world, for I believe that the office is the Christian's "Last Frontier."

Many will say that the principles contained herein are too simplistic and imply responsibilities that God will not undertake for the individual. But Jesus said, "Except you become as a little child, you shall not enter the kingdom of

Heaven." Simplicity and childlike trust have always been the mark of God's people, while unfathomable complexity and unequaled ability have always been the mark of God himself. For the child of God, the adventure into his Father's remarkable truths is both exciting and challenging. Furthermore, I do not ask that you believe *me* as you read this material, but that you believe the Word of God; unerring, infallible, and wholly practical.

For too long, we have worshiped at the shrine of our own intelligence and have assumed responsibilities God never intended us to shoulder. It is time for us to lay our self-imposed burdens down and take up our cross, allowing the Lordship of Christ to be made manifest in our lives, *particularly* at work.

It is my prayer that this material will assist you in fulfilling, in your life, Paul's admonition to Timothy:

Study to shew thyself approved unto God, a *workman* that needeth not to be ashamed, rightly dividing the word of truth. (2 Tim. 2:15; italics mine)

THE
CHRISTIAN
EMPLOYEE

CHAPTER ONE

The Monday Morning Mulligrubs Syndrome

John closes his Bible and sips the last of his coffee. He hesitates a moment before calling it a day. He listens to the sounds of his children saying their prayers as his wife puts them to bed. He hears the gentle pleasant sounds of the bedtime routines and the whispered "good nights."

John has a sense of genuine satisfaction, of having a fulfilled life. He, his wife and children are now a happy family. They have been Christians now for two years and their home, now mended, is a testimony to God's goodness. *Life is good*, John says to himself.

He reflects on the weekend with gladness in his heart. He finished many of the odd jobs he had been trying to get done for several weeks. He even had time to play tennis with his next-door neighbor—who, John recalls, has begun to show interest in a better way of life and has even asked questions about God.

And today, Sunday, has been a perfect day. All day long John and his wife have experienced a closeness and communion with God and a fresh awareness of His love. The Sunday school lesson gave John some new ideas for studying a topic in the Bible during the coming week. The sermon in the morning worship service was excellent and the congregation seemed alive with the presence of God.

But as John heads for bed, his thoughts turn to Monday. John sighs. Another work week ahead. He suddenly remembers the report that is due in the morning. He recalls the sharp criticism leveled by his boss toward the office staff lately, and the mountain of work that faces him in the morning. By the time John climbs into bed, a mild depression has moved in on him like a fog.

When John gets up the next morning, the fog has turned to pea soup.

"I'll never meet that deadline this week," he laments to his wife as he eats breakfast. "And Frank won't be able to carry his share of the load. He's been on another binge.

"And on top of that," he sighs as his mood becomes blacker with each passing moment, "we are about to start a special project. Why can't Mr. Taylor see that we're already swamped?

"Of course," he tells his wife for the third time in a week, "I wouldn't be having these problems if I had transferred to the sales department. I'd have more freedom and a better salary.

"Maybe," he concludes as he trudges toward the door, "I should have taken that job in Seattle last year after all."

Already he wishes today were Saturday. Already he is looking forward to the sanctuary of another weekend.

Our friend John is suffering from a common Christian ailment—the Monday Morning Mulligrubs. To John, work seems to be a plan perpetrated by the world to rob him of the good life he enjoys on the weekends. After all, work *is* basically unspiritual. "But," John sighs, "we *have* to work."

Meanwhile, John's ailment goes undiagnosed and as each

Monday rolls around, he suffers anew. John, like most Christians, believes that work is necessary and even honorable, since a man is supposed to support his family and is worse than a derelict if he doesn't. But at the same time, he believes that the system of secular employment is at enmity with the spiritual world. His only hope is that one day the system will be replaced by the millennium, so he sighs, "Maranatha; even so, come quickly, Lord Jesus." He wants the Lord to return so that he can escape the office.

Because he does not realize that he has an ailment, John does not seek a cure for the Monday Morning Mulligrubs, which we will call the MMM Syndrome.

Strangely, we Christians are more likely to have problems with employment than are non-Christians. We have experienced the sweet communion with God that is available to man. We know the joys of being a husband and father under God. The non-Christian, on the other hand, is more likely to view work as his primary source of personal achievement and satisfaction. He is much less likely to enjoy his family. To him, his worth as a family man is measured by the size of his paycheck, his social status, and the college his children will attend.

As Christians, stamped with the nature of God, we don't enjoy going to the office five days a week to work with non-Christians, who *aren't* stamped with the divine nature. The people, the pressure, the whole environment of the secular office combine to burst our spiritual bubble of peace and joy.

But we *have* to work, and so we suffer on . . . and on. . . .

The Spiritual Nervous System

Our bodies were created with a highly complex nervous system. This intricate system carries impulses which inform us not only of physical pleasure but also of pain and

3

impending danger, such as a developing disease. If you are developing an ulcer, your nervous system tells you that something is wrong in your stomach. It informs you that you have a pain in your stomach. Or if you accidentally place your hand on the hot element of a stove, your nervous system, acting on "red alert," tells you to remove your hand—immediately. We could not survive without this intricate system.

We also have a spiritual nervous system designed to inform us of the pleasures of serving God and to warn us of spiritual danger. It is through our spiritual system that God tells us "do this" or "don't do that." He warns us when we are playing with fire or when we have a spiritual disease that needs attention.

When our spiritual nervous system sounds an alarm, it is God tapping us on the shoulder, trying to draw our attention to a certain ailment. The depression which John developed on Sunday night was just such a warning signal, a pain which warned that something was wrong.

What do we do when we experience a bothersome, frequent physical pain? We go to the doctor, of course, for diagnosis and treatment. We wouldn't dare ignore a serious pain. When we have spiritual pains, we should go to God for diagnosis and treatment. A human doctor might tell us to go home, learn to live with the pain because there is nothing he can do. But our Physician, who is no less than Almighty God, offers a solution to every illness.

We Christians are ingenious when it comes to devising excuses for our spiritual diseases. If we ignored our physical diseases as we do our spiritual ones, we'd all be in the grave. We say, "Well, we can't live on the mountaintop all the time . . ." or "I guess the excitement of being a Christian wears off after a while . . ." or even "It looks like God wants me to bear this. . . ." But these attitudes aren't scriptural. Jesus said we should have "abundant life," joy that is *full*, and peace like a *river*. When we are depressed about work, don't enjoy our jobs and the people we work with, then our spiritual nervous systems are telling us that we have a disease. That disease robs us of the abundant life, the full joy, and the flowing peace.

The Plan

Essentially, the entire thrust of the Bible is to instruct mankind to establish a vital relationship with God. Its secondary thrust is to instruct us to form relationships with each other. God wants us to relate to our fellowman *properly*. Within the family of man are different groups to which we are to relate in different ways.

In Ephesians 5 and 6, God has given us a list of those relationships with instructions for each. In giving us this list, God has also shown us what our priorities should be. First and most important is the God-man relationship, then man-man, then wife-husband, husband-wife, children-parents, parents-children, and then servant-master relationships.

Consider for a moment how much instruction we have received on each. God has led us into a deeper understanding of our relationships in the church and in the family. But how much instruction have we received on employment, the "servant" relationship? We may hear a sermon once a year on how good hard work is for the soul, but that has been the extent of it. God has followed His own list of priorities in Ephesians 5 and 6 in restoring the church today, and now I believe He is leading us into a deeper understanding of employment.

But why? God isn't interested in our mundane, unspiritual 8 to 5 jobs, is He? Oh, but He is. He actually has a plan for the whole system of secular employment. He actually wants us to be victorious *at* the office and *over* the office. Again, why? Because He, the living God who drew us into His kingdom, wants to draw all those people at the office into His kingdom also—all the Jims and Janes and Toms, the caustic bosses and the alcoholic colleagues.

Millions of people all over the world on every continent are without the knowledge of God. At the same time, millions of people all over the world *have* the knowledge of God. Those millions of lost people go to work every day with those millions of Christians. Think about the significance of this for a moment.

We are in that age of world-wide harvesting to which Jesus referred when He said, "The harvest truly is plenteous, but the labourers are few. Pray ye therefore the Lord of the harvest, that he will send forth labourers into his harvest" (Matt. 9:37-38).

God views you as a laborer to reap at your office. He is sending you out to that "patch" of people He wants harvested for His kingdom. But, you may say, "laborers" mean evangelists, preachers, and missionaries.

But look at Frank, the alcoholic in your office. He won't go to a revival. He won't go to a Christian businessmen's organization. He won't go to a prayer meeting. He won't even watch an evangelist on television. So, where will he go? Where does he *have* to go? To the office. As for you, you won't go bar-hopping. You won't go to a stag party. You won't play golf on Sunday morning during church time. But where do you *have* to go to associate with non-Christians? The office.

If we had our way, we would live Sunday every day. If Frank had his way, he would live Saturday night every day. We both would be completely content to totally separate ourselves from each other.

But God had another plan. Jesus prayed that we be in the

world, but not of the world. His prayer has been answered. God has arranged it so that we *have* to be in the world. He has made *sure* we will be in the world, because He knows that if we had a choice, we would never go out into all the world five days a week, eight hours a day. He has arranged the system so that we are stuck with Frank and Frank with us.

God has also arranged that Christians and non-Christians be forced together under the worst possible conditions. It is easy to be a light shining in the darkness when you and Frank get together at a barbecue or a Sunday afternoon visit or on a fishing trip. In an atmosphere of relaxation, good food, family togetherness, and good moods, it's easy to feel good about life, as John did on Sunday night. It's easy to hold your temper when nothing goes wrong. But to be a light shining in the darkness of pressurized work conditions—deadlines, sales quotas, incompetent bosses, flaring tempers—is a different matter. Yet this too is a part of God's plan. You may feel good about life at a barbecue—but so does Frank. You may be kind and patient with people in a relaxed atmosphere—but so is Frank. It's only when the heat's on that the difference between Christians and non-Christians can clearly emerge. That's why God always has the thermostat turned up at the office.

Never before have lives been so empty. And never before have such vast numbers of people been *employed*. Before the technological boom of the twentieth century, the majority of workers in the world were employed in small factories or shops, or had small independent businesses. The growth of the economy in our generation is phenomenal. It is the age of super-conglomerates and 5,000-employee factories. It is an age of travel when a Christian can be exposed to more people in one day than a Christian a hundred years ago could meet in a year.

But again, lives have never been so empty.

The harvest is ripe. God is right on schedule. And we are the key to His plan of harvesting.

God wants us at the office—we can accept that much. He wants us to associate with Frank—we can accept that too. But is there more? Does God want us to feel stuck with Frank? Do we just grit our teeth and bear him, while we try to *act* like Christians?

God has a better way.

CHAPTER TWO

Which Side of the Bed?

An employee spends approximately sixty-three percent of his waking hours at work or on work-related activities. Because, then, of the impact our lives can have on others, we need to examine our relationships with the non-Christians at the office.

Most Christians point a finger at the people they work with, blaming them for the miserable and unspiritual atmosphere at the office. We have all thought how wonderful it would be if everyone at work were a Christian. And, in fact, most of our problems and complaints about our jobs do, directly or indirectly, involve other people.

Take a look at your own job situation. Do you really dislike construction or bookkeeping or teaching or selling? Write down all your complaints about work. Don't almost all of them involve people—the boss, the secretary, the colleague? People themselves are the single worst irritant we face at work. The real problem, we rightly conclude, is that we must work with non-Christians. They don't like to talk about the Lord, they tell dirty jokes, they continually plot and scheme behind the boss's back, and, in general, keep things stirred up all the time.

Although there is a natural strain between the Christian and the non-Christian, what would happen if we had good relationships with one another? What would happen if you actually had a good relationship with Frank? Are we supposed to have good relationships with nonbelievers? Yes. In fact, good relationships are crucial to both God's harvesting plan and to our own happiness as an employee.

Forming Relationships

One need only read a few chapters of any of the Gospels to see how thoroughly Jesus associated with people whom we would call "unchristian." He seemed to go out of His way to eat with tax collectors, common fishermen, and even the man He knew would betray Him. He had good relationships with all kinds of people. *Relationship* means a state of being connected.

We are to be actually *connected* to people. But we can be connected in a constructive way or a destructive way. Let's examine the mechanics of relationships to understand how people connect with one another.

The Cycle

A relationship is determined by three factors, which operate in a cycle. These three factors are: attitudes, actions, and circumstances. Each person lives in a cycle. We face a circumstance, form an attitude about it, and that attitude in turn governs what we do—our actions. That action in turn produces

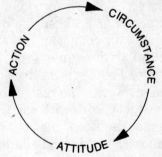

another circumstance, either for ourselves or others. When two people meet and associate for any length of time, their cycles interact, and a relationship, good, bad or indifferent, is formed.

Joe goes to work one day feeling just great. Everything is going well for him. But when he arrives at the office, the boss calls everyone together to announce that the company is in very poor financial condition and some of the employees will have to be laid off. Joe has only in the past year earned an income he considers satisfactory and now he may lose it. He reacts to that circumstance by forming an attitude—dread.

He struggles through the day, but cannot keep his mind on his work. He worries about the family. What kind of Christmas will they have? How far will their savings go? Who will be laid off first? Certainly George and Tom should go first. How much are the monthly bills? He remembers all those charge accounts, but can't recall how much money is due on them. Well, Joe decides, they simply have to start cutting back—immediately.

At five-twenty that evening, Joe arrives home. As he walks in the back door, the first sight to meet his eyes is the groceries his wife has just brought home. Today, he remembers, is shopping day. He counts the number of bags on the kitchen table—eight of them. Joe grumbles to himself. He rummages through the bags and finds a large roast, olives, a bottle of cooking wine, a gallon of ice cream. . . .

Just then Gloria comes to greet him.

"Hi, honey! Did you have a nice day?" she asks cheerfully as she begins to put the groceries away.

"Gloria, do we really need all this stuff? That roast would feed an army! Don't you follow a budget? We can't afford all this; you're spending too. . . ." He pauses just long enough to find the ticket for the groceries, "$84.29!"

"You know I don't follow a budget—we've never followed a budget," Gloria snaps. "You're the one who insists on roast beef *almost every night* of the week—so don't criticize me! Besides, you tell me just to buy what I want. . . ."

"That's the trouble! You buy what you want and you aren't the one who has to worry about paying for it! You aren't the one who slaves at the office all day. Where do you think all that money comes from?"

"Just a minute! Don't talk to me about slaving! You just try washing and cleaning and cooking all day and driving the kids back and forth about five times a day and then tell me about slaving!"

"I'm the one who pays the bills around here so I have the right to tell you what to buy!"

"And I don't have any rights?"

From there, Joe and Gloria go on and on. Gloria reminds Joe of that expensive fishing rod he bought last week. Joe informs her that he will *use* that fishing rod after all that coming weekend instead of taking her out to dinner as they had already planned.

Let's look at what happened to this relationship. When Joe learned that he might lose his job, he panicked. When he got home, his attitude of fear became an action—confronting Gloria about the groceries. Gloria, who had no idea why Joe was upset, since he had never told her what had happened at work, formed an attitude about the circumstance Joe had presented to her—she was angry. Her attitude instantly expressed itself. Her anger created a new circumstance for Joe and so it went, escalating with each new turn of the cycle, until their relationship that day and possibly throughout the rest of the week was in shambles.

A diagram of their interaction would look like this:

Which Side of the Bed?

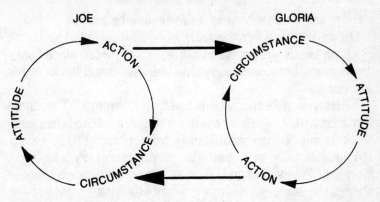

All relationships are formed in this way. This process occurs at work with the boss and co-workers even though the actions may not be as overt as they are at home. An angry action at the office might be slamming a door or sulking, instead of yelling like Joe and Gloria at home.

"As a man thinketh in his heart, so is he." The phrase "as a man *thinketh* in his heart" describes our *attitudes;* the phrase "so *is* he" describes our *actions*. What we think in our hearts (an attitude) will invariably manifest itself in action. If the attitude is anger, that anger will appear in some action. If the attitude is love, the actions will be love. It is impossible to hide the attitudes—they will show in some way, however subtle.

The action, then, is only the outward results of the attitude. The problem lies with the attitude itself. Our attitudes, which we sometimes call moods, are in a constant state of change. It is because of these fluctuations that a person can get out of bed one morning feeling great but has to force himself out of bed the very next morning because he feels lousy .

On mornings when he feels great he sings in the shower, whistles on his way downstairs, kisses his wife good morning, compliments his secretary, performs his duties gladly, and pleasantly greets everyone he meets.

On mornings when he feels lousy, he throws the alarm clock on the floor, snarls at his wife, grumbles all the way downstairs, complains about his breakfast, and barks at his secretary.

What was different about the two mornings? The home environment, his wife's cooking, the mechanics of the alarm clock do not change significantly from morning to morning. He presumably still had the same secretary the next morning. What changed? The attitude. The alarm clock is always the same—it *always* presents us with an unpleasant circumstance; it is the constantly changing human attitude that causes us to react to the clock differently.

Understanding the cycle of attitudes-actions-circumstances is crucial to our Christian lives. We must understand that the attitude is the problem, not the actions or the circumstances.

Why is this so important? It doesn't matter if we have bad moods. Everyone gets up on the wrong side of the bed sometimes. Right?

The Chain Reaction

Joe and Gloria sit down and talk that evening after supper. Joe explains what happened at work. Together they plan a course of financial discipline and then stay up to watch the Johnny Carson Show. Their relationship is mended.

The next morning, they oversleep. Joe jumps out of bed at seven-twenty-five, stubs his toe on the bed shakes Gloria frantically to awaken her—she has to get the children up—and dashes off for the bathroom. He can't find the shaving lather. After turning the bathroom upside down, he remembers that the kids used it to make a face on the trunk of the car yesterday. When he finally tracks it down, he cuts himself in two places while shaving.

Which Side of the Bed?

Downstairs, seated at the kitchen table, he immediately begins to pat his foot impatiently (the same foot he stubbed on the bed). He watches Gloria dashing madly around the kitchen, now trying to butter the toast with one hand and pour milk with the other. Johnny can't find his spelling book and Suzie has lost her favorite hairclip and the school bus is due in ten minutes. Joe looks irritably at his watch three times in the course of one minute. And he begins to think.

"If that woman would only get up on time, we could enjoy a leisurely breakfast together. She knows I hate to gulp down my food . . . and this isn't the first time it's happened either." The more he pursues this line of thought, the more irritated he becomes. Finally, he feels that he *has* to say something. This is, after all, a perfect time to point out some of her inefficiencies, since she is in the very act of demonstrating them.

"Honey, I really love you, but if you would just get up on time, we could have a pleasant breakfast together." Just then she throws the plate down in front of him. The eggs are sort of stiff and the toast is moderately burned. "*Then,* you wouldn't be so rushed and my eggs and toast wouldn't be burned. You keep this house in an uproar!" At that moment, the carpool arrives and Joe jumps up, grabs his briefcase and swoops out the door like an angry tornado.

Joe dives in the car, thinking about the fact that here he goes again without any breakfast. He begins to complain to his friends. They had been carrying on typical carpool conversation and naturally, one of them has a ready quip about Joe's situation. They begin to needle him in fun. To Joe, however, the jokes only add insult to the injury of his empty stomach. Without warning, Joe snaps at his friends. Everyone falls into silence.

Let us pause here a moment. Joe is in a bad mood. His day has started all wrong. Already relationships are damaged.

THE CHRISTIAN EMPLOYEE

He has hurt Gloria's feelings and ruined her morning. She feels unfairly accused and she is bruised. We will call her Casualty # 1. The friends in the carpool have felt the sting of Joe's sharp tongue and they get out of the car at the office still smarting. They are Casualties # 2, # 3, and # 4. And Joe hasn't even gotten to work yet! But his bad mood wreaks still more havoc.

As he opens the door to his office at 8:03, he remembers that report which is due for the staff meeting at nine. "No problem," he thinks to himself, "I've finished most of it. I have time to get the last two or three pages written and typed up." He heads straight for his secretary, Peggy.

"Don't forget that report we've got to finish this morning. It's due at nine, you know. I'll bring the last two pages in a few minutes." He turns on his heels and disappears into his office.

A few minutes later, Peggy appears at the door. She looks a little strained and green around the gills.

"Uh, sir, uh, don't *you* have the report?" She quickly adds, "Don't you remember that I gave it back to you typed up yesterday afternoon?"

"But I gave it back again! I laid it right on top of your typewriter."

Frantically the two of them tear up their offices looking for the report. At nine, they give up.

As Joe leaves for the staff meeting, he lets his secretary know just how inefficient she is. "I've told you a hundred times to keep your desk straight! You have to learn to keep papers in certain places so you can find them!"

Joe is an efficiency expert, you see. He has had three one-hour courses in management at the local university and now he is an expert on organization. As he strides off down the hall to the meeting, he leaves Peggy shaking, stewing, and hurting.

Which Side of the Bed?

Peggy—Casualty # 5.

The boss, a very competent individual, takes his seat at the staff table. Noting with satisfaction that it is precisely nine, he calls the meeting to order. As he is informing the staff of the importance of this meeting, Joe enters, out of breath, and takes his seat awkwardly under the boss's steady glare.

"Joe," the boss begins, "we need to hear your report first. The decisions we make today will depend largely upon the findings of your study."

Joe just hangs his head. "Sir, it's not *quite* ready."

The boss looks over his glasses at Joe.

"Well, sir, we, uh, had some, uh, difficulties this morning with. . . ." He falls into silence.

The meeting continues, obviously floundering. The boss makes several pointed references to the fact that decisions cannot be made because Joe didn't have his report ready.

When the meeting is over, the boss calls Joe aside to tell him just how inefficient *he* is. And the next time, he informs Joe, he expects him to have the report ready and to be on time. Inefficiency, he emphasizes, is inexcusable.

Joe has reaped what he sowed, a spiritual law which operates as surely as the natural law of gravity. Joe himself—Casualty # 6.

Joe manages to get through the day in one piece, but he continues in the same pattern of behavior until five o'clock. Now, however, let's go back to visit all those people he left in his wake as he plowed through the morning.

As Gloria washes the breakfast dishes, she fumes over Joe's harsh accusations. It was Joe, she recalls, who kept her up late watching the Johnny Carson Show. Jimmy lost one of his books and *she* was the one who had to find it—Joe doesn't have to cope with all these little problems that come up.

THE CHRISTIAN EMPLOYEE

A neighbor calls on the telephone. Would Gloria mind keeping the dog inside on Mondays and Thursdays until after the garbage man has come? "My lawn is covered with garbage," the neighbor explains. "Dogs will be dogs you know!"

That does it! Gloria proceeds to tell her neighbor that it is none of her business *when* she puts her dog out and all she has to do is secure the garbage can lid better. Gloria slams down the receiver.

The neighbor—Casualty # 7.

After Joe had snapped at them—the friends in the carpool go through their days snapping at the parking lot attendants, the elevator operators, and their wives. Estimated Casualties—# 8 through # 20!

Then Peggy's husband calls to ask how her day is going and to ask if he can invite Mr. Smith home for dinner that night. She flies into him, accusing him of thoughtless selfishness. "I have enough to do without having to cook for guests! You never think about *me*!"

The husband and everyone *he* contacts—Casualties # 21 through # 25.

Gloria's neighbor calls her husband at work to tell him how rude Gloria was. The husband becomes angry and declares that he will never invite *them* to his Saturday afternoon barbecues any more.

And so on and on it goes. And it can all be traced back to how Joe got out of the bed that morning. Joe's bad mood set up a chain reaction that mushroomed into an emotional holocaust. And the picture is even more complex than we have described here. If you throw a stone into a lake, it sets up waves. But if you throw a handful of stones into the water, the whole surface becomes disturbed. If, for example, one out of every four people in a city of 200,000 gets up in a foul mood, you can imagine what a fearful matter the results would be! Each day, we go out into the world with other people and play a kind of human bumper-car, each person reacting to circumstances in a vicious cycle of attitudes-actions-circumstances.

If it were possible to trace the ultimate effects of each of Joe's actions throughout the day to their completion, we would be astonished. Some poor taxicab driver on the other side of town would be chewed out that day by a grouchy passenger who somehow bumped into someone who bumped into someone who bumped into Joe.

Do you think this is an exaggeration? Our ordinary bad moods couldn't possibly have such a vast and destructive effect on so many lives—could they?

Ten Little Israelites—and Then There Were None (Numbers 16)

One day, while the children of Israel were out camping in the desert, not long after being delivered from slavery in Egypt, one of the Israelites, named Korah, was sitting in his tent in a foul mood. This particular man was *always* in a foul mood.

Two good friends, Abiram and Dathan, drop in for a visit. The three of them pull up lawn chairs outside the tent to enjoy the desert scenery and catch up on local news. Eventually, the conversation comes around to politics.

"This guy, Moses," Korah remarks, "is something else. He really believes he is special. He even thinks God picked him out to lead us! He isn't even a priest. And doesn't he know that all the people of Israel are chosen? We are all anointed! Who is he to exalt himself over us like this?"

"Yeah," Dathan agrees, "he thinks he's better than we are."

The three of them talk further and conclude that a better leader than Moses should be found to direct the nation.

Moses simply isn't capable. They dissect all his mistakes and recount the reasons why he isn't qualified.

"In the first place," Korah says, "Moses is a foreigner—he was raised in the palace of the Egyptian Pharaoh from infancy. How could he possibly understand the people of Israel?" Abiram and Dathan nod their heads solemnly in agreement.

"Furthermore," Korah continues, "he is actually a murderer! Did you know that? Yes, he murdered an Egyptian in cold blood! Well, then he had to flee for his life. Why, he spent most of his life tending sheep on the back side of nowhere."

"And, of course," they agree, "Moses is responsible for the disastrous situation we are in now, wandering around out in the desert. If he had exerted proper leadership, we would be in the Promised Land, enjoying milk and honey right now, instead of suffering on this miserable diet—wild birds and that awful bread that appears on the grass every once in a while. But then, Moses is accustomed to the desert life. He has no idea of the life style and security we enjoyed in Egypt."

It became readily apparent to them that while Moses was the worst possible choice of leaders, they themselves would be the best possible. Each of them had been born and raised among the people. Each of them was well known and active in civic, social and religious affairs. They also—and this was most important—were in touch with the people. They had their fingers on the pulse beat of the nation.

So Korah, Abiram, and Dathan start a grassroots campaign. Early the next morning, they make rounds of the tribes, politicking and mudslinging. By nine o'clock, they have *250 of the most respected men of the nation* behind them. Together, they go see Moses. Their party, "Masses against Moses," confronts Moses and asks him to step down or be impeached.

Moses is not intimidated in the least. "We'll see about this, Korah," he says. "We will appear together before the tabernacle in the morning and ask God which one of us He wants to be leader of the nation."

Korah was surprised by this reaction. After all, Korah had a lot of clout behind him—Moses should have trembled before the 250 national leaders. But he didn't. So Korah sets about campaigning further until, by the next morning, he has the *whole nation* of Israel supporting him. Korah, you see, believes that strength lies in numbers. "Surely any leader who has the entire populace behind him will be approved by God," Korah says to himself.

In the morning, all the tribes come to the tabernacle to rally behind Korah. Moses has only Aaron voting for him. The two lone men wait for an answer from God. God does answer. He tells Moses to move out of the way—He is going to wipe the nation of Israel off the face of the earth.

But Moses and Aaron protest and ask God for mercy. God replies that He will destroy only the three ringleaders and their families. Moses and Aaron run through the crowd, warning everyone, until within moments, the three men and their households are left standing alone.

Suddenly, the ground opens up under Korah, Abiram, and Dathan and swallows the three families. While the people are still gasping over what they have just seen, fire comes down out of heaven and kills the 250 leaders who first sided with Korah.

After this amazing display of God's power and wrath, the people affirm Moses as leader of the nation. The rebellion is quenched and everything is back to normal, right? Wrong.

The attitude of rebellion has already infected the nation. The *very next day* rumblings and complaints against Moses are heard once again. And again God takes action against the rebels. He sends a plague in which 14,700 people die.

Look at what has happened in a time period of *three days*. Korah infected Abiram and Dathan; those three infected 250 more; those 253 together infected the whole nation. It started with Korah, Abiram and Dathan grumbling and it ended with the funerals of 14,953 people.

And all in three days' time.

One man can indeed affect his entire city or even nation. We cannot hold lightly the impact our lives have upon others. Korahs are at work in the world every day, in politics, offices, churches and homes. Korah starts complaining and within a *short* period of time, that government or church or home or office is in an uproar.

Paul wrote that a *little* leaven leavens the whole loaf. A small amount of leaven affects the whole mass of dough. This describes the negative side of our impact upon others. We can have a positive effect also. Jesus said, *"One* candle gives light to the *whole* house."

Most of us never see the far-reaching effects of our lives. We never hear about the poor taxicab driver on the other side of town. We never hear about the store clerks or secretaries or neighbors or elevator operators who were defiled by our bad moods. But I believe that God is going to reveal them to us in time.

The waves we set up by our foul moods *will* run their natural course, unless they are deliberately interrupted. Human nature acts as a conductor, passing the current along to the next person. The waves normally meet no resistance, but flow easily from person to person. You can observe this yourself in the laboratory of life. The next time you hear a person in line at the airport or grocery store or in any situation where people feel inconvenienced make a harsh remark, watch the faces of the people around that person.

You can see the poison spread. The cycle occurs just as predictably as any law of nature. It is the law of man. It is as though people are trapped in the cycle of human nature, unable to break out. And they are.

We Christians, too, operate in the cycle of attitude-action-circumstance. We don't understand why we still get angry or hurt. After all, we have been born again and are new creatures. We sometimes get along with Harry and Bill on the job, but we just as often don't. They can't damage our salvation, but they sure can put a dent in our joy. Harry makes a remark that we don't like and we react. Suddenly our joy has vanished. But while they can't win us to their way of life, we can't win them to the Lord either. It's a stand-off and a miserable one at that.

What we need is to break the cycle. God offers us a way to do that.

CHAPTER THREE

Getting to the Heart
of the Matter

Have you looked closely at the lives of the apostles? As moderns, we look back two thousand years and think, "Oh, how exciting it must have been to have lived in the times of the early church." But consider the specific information recorded in the Scriptures. Paul, for example, was beaten frequently, thrown into prison, shipwrecked, and even rejected by his own Christian brothers. One might even say that Paul was "snake-bit." So intense were his tribulations that at one point he even despaired of life (2 Cor. 1:8). In the lives of early Christians, tribulations were the rule rather than the exception. Yet they still lived abundant lives.

How did Paul and the other early Christians maintain supernatural joy in the midst of persecution and hardship? When Jesus prayed for His followers, both contemporary and future ones, He prayed, "I pray not that thou [God] shouldest take them out of the world . . . as thou has sent me into the world, even so have I sent them into the world." It was Jesus' will that we be thrust out into the abrasive conditions and circumstances of the world. Just prior to this prayer, however, Jesus said to His disciples, "These things I have spoken unto you, that in me ye might have peace. In the world ye shall have tribulation: but be of good cheer; I have overcome the world" (John 16:33).

Jesus was despised, rejected, threatened, cursed, mocked, then beaten, humiliated, betrayed, and executed in the most painful method of the day, yet He said, "I have conquered. I have overcome." And He did not say this *after* the resurrection but as He was facing the cross.

Jesus also told us that in Him we might have peace. This peace was not automatic. But the *potential* for it was real. We have to obtain it. How? By overcoming. Overcoming what? *Circumstances*. The world gives peace through agreeable circumstances. Jesus' peace has nothing to do with outward circumstances. It is the kind of peace "that no man taketh from you" (John 16:22).

This was the secret the early Christians had. They had the peace of God, and could, therefore, rejoice in the face of beatings, stonings, and prison. The stripes on their bruised backs had no effect on the peace in their hearts.

With an eye to obtain this peace that passes understanding, let's look once more at the attitude-action-circumstance cycle. We have seen that actions are born in the attitudes and attitudes are formed by circumstances.

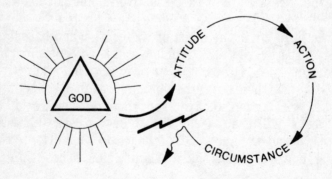

God does not change our circumstances to suit us, but instead wants to change us to suit our circumstances, that is, to so change us as to render our circumstances of no effect. To do this, He must change our attitudes. He must break the cycle of human nature that keeps us literally going around in circles spiritually.

God's power working to change our attitudes is the day-to-day reality of Christianity. When we reach the point that our attitudes are molded solely by God and not by outward circumstances, then our resulting attitudes will produce godly actions. The sting is removed from circumstances. Then we will be overcomers. We will be Christ-like and will have the mind of Christ.

Jesus is saying to us, "Be of good cheer. It can be done!"

The Blood and the Word

When a person wants to establish a relationship with Christ, he must be willing to confess his sins to God. But it cannot stop there. Jesus said, "Ye must be born again." When we confess our sins, God forgives us and the slate is wiped clean. But if the relationship stops there, the slate is quickly dirtied again. Nothing has changed in that person.

God is more interested in *why* we sin than in the sins themselves. It is the source of the sin that God wants to reveal to us. And what is the source of our actions? Attitudes.

If a person is not willing to have God deal with his attitudes, then he is not willing to accept Jesus as Lord. God demands that we be willing to have our hearts explored. He requires that we give Him permission to change our basic, root attitudes.

Therefore, after a person confesses his sins, he must also confess his attitudes, his nature. First, he confesses "I have sinned" (actions). Now he confesses "I am a sinner" (attitudes). That says something about his very being, his character. It is a much more difficult confession to make. But only when he has confessed both his actions (sin) and his attitudes (sinner), is a person ready to enter into a vital relationship with Christ.

Jesus always responds to such confessions and pleas for mercy. "Behold, I stand at the door and knock. If any man hear my voice and open the door, I will come in and sup with him and he with me." When this occurs, the Spirit of Christ takes up residence within the person. Spiritual rebirth has taken place. God has given that person a new nature and eternal life. For this purpose did Jesus go to the cross.

But that is only the beginning.

In describing the man without Christ, the Bible uses terms such as "the old man," "the natural man," or "the carnal man." These terms express the condition of the person who is a sinner. When the person is born again, a new nature is now alive within him. But the old man is still alive and well within him also. The old and new natures become roommates and that inevitably means war.

As long as life does not present any issues on which the new and old natures disagree, things roll along smoothly. But when a circumstance arises where Christ and the old man differ, inner conflict erupts. If Christ wins the argument, the outward action is godly and inner peace is restored. If the old man wins, the outward actions will be ungodly and inner turmoil (from the conscience) results. Every action mirrors its source, revealing whether Christ or the old man won the argument.

One Scripture asks, "Can two walk together except they be agreed?" You cannot walk with God if the old man always wins the disputes. You cannot walk with the world if Jesus reigns. Another Scripture reads, "There is a way which seemeth right unto a man, but the end thereof are the ways of death." The old man will choose a way that immediately pleases him, an action that appeals to him at the moment. But the accumulative result of a life ruled by "what seemeth right unto a man" is destruction.

The old and new natures will continue to war for a time. The old man will often demand and get his way. Sin results, for which God has prescribed remedies.

"If we confess our sins, he [God] is faithful and just to forgive us, and cleanse us from all unrighteousness." God will do *two* things for us if we confess our sins. He will *forgive* and *cleanse*.

Forgiveness comes only through the atoning blood of Christ. "This is my blood of the new testament, which is shed for many for the remission of sins" (Matt. 26:28). Cleansing, on the other hand, comes only by the Word of God. "Wherewithal shall a young man cleanse his way? by taking heed thereto according to thy word" (Ps. 119:9). Forgiveness and cleansing, then, have different functions. Forgiveness, by the blood of Christ, is for our sins (actions). Cleansing, by taking heed to the Word of God, is for our nature (attitudes). Jesus said to His disciples, "Now ye are *clean through the word* which I have spoken to you."

Spiritual Problem	Remedy	Cleansing Agent
Actions ("I have sinned")	Forgiveness	Blood of Christ
Attitudes ("I am a sinner")	Cleansing	Word of God

This process, blood for our sins and the Word for our nature, our character, is God's way of maturing us. By forgiveness and cleansing He slowly closes the gap between what we are and what we should be. When we face an unpleasant circumstance, we form an attitude, perhaps, "I don't like this situation at all. I'm going to let somebody have a piece of my mind!" God's attitude would be perhaps, "All things work for good to those who love Me!" What a contrast between our attitudes and God's attitudes. We see circumstance; He sees the plan.

It is just this contrast between our attitudes and God's attitudes (principles) that causes defeat, spiritual pain, and our poor relationships with others. It is this discrepancy that causes our spiritual diseases. When you and God disagree about how to respond to a certain circumstance, something has to give, and you can be sure that it's not going to be Him. You are the one who has to give in to Him. When God deals with our basic, gut-level attitudes, He is tampering with our very selves and it will hurt. We won't like it at all. He will be shining a light into a cave that has never been exposed to light before.

Something will begin to happen, though, as you allow God to gradually put your attitudes into line with His. The old man, that petty tyrant who used to stomp and strut and demand the fulfillment of his every whim, will become quieter and quieter. He will become sickly and pale. The new nature will become more and more the real you. As you become Christ-like, with the mind of Christ, those strained relationships will gradually ease. And those constant fluctuations of the attitudes of the heart will cease.

Constancy, based on the Word of God and the person of Jesus, is the name of the game. The power of Christianity lies in the reality of the relationship between a person and the King of kings. Jesus is steadfast, and therefore, in Him, we become 'steadfast. He is constant, so we can become constant. He is love, and we can become love. All this depends, however, upon our choosing to exchange our own attitudes for His.

If you wake up one morning and say, "Lord Jesus, I love you," you expect and may sense His answer, "I'm so glad. I love you too." What if, however, the next morning you approach Him the same way, only to hear Him say, "Get away from me. I don't feel good this morning." That's unimaginable, isn't it? Or could you picture the Father and Son arguing? No. The Father, the Son, and the Spirit are always in perfect agreement and unity. They never have bad moods, bad attitudes, or fluctuations in their personalities. And because Christ is *in* us, we have the potential for the *same* stability He has.

There is no instant maturity for the Christian. Everyone must go through the process of forgiveness and cleansing, always with the attitude, "Lord, show me. I'm willing." You can't matriculate without going through the school of the Holy Ghost.

God has given us principles for every conceivable aspect of life. Not surprisingly, then, He has given us a set of principles concerning our employment. As we examine these principles, let's allow God to show us where our attitudes are wrong and then allow Him to mold our attitudes to conform with His. It is hard to change lifelong attitudes, but it is also highly rewarding.

And it's a sure cure for the Monday Morning Mulligrubs.

CHAPTER FOUR

The Author and the Finisher

The most severe symptom of the Monday Morning Syndrome is blurred vision, spiritual astigmatism which distorts our perspective. God said, "Where there is no *vision*, my people perish." Many Christians today have a mental image of a terrible battle occurring between the forces of good and evil.

As we watch the evening news on television or read the evening newspaper, we often shake our heads and sigh, "What is the world coming to?" On every front, evil seems to be winning. And in truth, Satan has marshaled all the forces of hell against the world, to envelop and destroy the kingdom of God.

But do we have a proper perspective of the battle? Is God's goodness losing the war? We hear a common expression, "Satan may win the battle, but God will win the war in the end." This knowledge may encourage us to endure, but is it really sufficient for the Christian in his daily life?

God, knowing the end from the beginning, is more interested in how we are doing in our own personal foxholes.

He is more concerned with the health and welfare of His troops than He is with Satan. God *knows* what the world is coming to—the return of His Son, Jesus.

We Christians, however, often feel that we have to leave the security of the camp and our fellow soldiers to journey alone and defenseless behind enemy lines—the office or the shop. We feel safer back in the camp, but we cannot have a victory without an enemy and a battle. Only after that will the camp be the site of a victory celebration.

In order to correct our vision, let's go back into history to view a remarkable event which occurred almost 2,600 years ago.

God's Graffiti

The setting for our study is found in the books of Jeremiah The nation of Israel, led by Jehoiakim, king of Judah, has gradually departed from serving God and is now in a state of gross immorality and idolatry. Through the prophet Jeremiah, God repeatedly warns Jehoiakim, but to no avail. Finally, Jeremiah prophesies that Israel will be overthrown by Nebuchadnezzar, the mighty king of Babylon. Not long afterward, this comes to pass. Israel is led as a nation of slaves into Babylon.

Babylon was a wonder of architecture. According to secular historians, the city was constructed in a square with sixty miles of perimeter and surrounded by walls two hundred feet high and eighty-seven to ninety feet thick. It has been said that four chariots could race side by side along the top of that great wall. Outside was a moat two hundred feet wide and ninety feet deep.

The builders of Babylon had constructed the city over the Euphrates River. The river ran through the center of the city, dividing it in half. The design insured a constant supply of fresh water in a part of the world where wells could run dry at the wrong moment.

The city was unassailable. It was impossible for an army of that day to break through or over the walls. The only way to gain entrance was by damming up the Euphrates and crawling under the walls in the river bed. But even this tactic had been anticipated. The builders had constructed two inner walls, running parallel to the banks of the river *inside* the city. If an enemy managed to crawl under the wall, he was faced by two inner walls as massive as the outer ones. Not only would he have failed to gain entrance, but he would, in fact, have been trapped in a canyon and easily slaughtered by the Babylonians.

The two inner walls had heavy gates at intervals to allow city residents access to the river to draw water. The gates were made of brass and secured by heavy bars of iron, an important detail, as we shall see. Each night, the inner gates were locked.

When Nebuchadnezzar became king, he secured the city even further. Realizing that his kingdom was still vulnerable to siege, he laid up a tremendous stock of provisions, enough to sustain the city for twenty years. In addition, the fabulous Hanging Gardens of Babylon were functionally designed to supply food—they were not simply a landscaping, beautification project. In case of siege, the city could live indefinitely off the produce of the Hanging Gardens, before having to touch the twenty-year supply.

Babylon, then, was a perfect city, absolutely secure and invulnerable. Brilliantly conceived, it had a constant fresh water supply, massive defenses, a virtually inexhaustible food supply, not to mention its arsenal and fierce army. It was breath-takingly beautiful and luxuriously wealthy. Modern cities rarely achieve the perfection and security of ancient Babylon.

To this magnificent city came the Israelites, chained and

dirty. They had lost the land which the Lord their God had given to them many centuries before—and they had lost it to a fierce, godless people. Even the house of God, the temple in Jerusalem had been destroyed and stripped of its sacred riches. The victors carried the people, all their possessions and all their national treasures back to their own land. The spoils of war were a matter of prestige and national pride. They were displayed and safeguarded in a warehouse that served as a bank or national treasury, and only in extreme financial emergencies would a nation sell them. Among the treasures that Nebuchadnezzar carried away from the temple in Jerusalem were the sacred vessels of the priesthood.

But God had a plan for His little tribe, which to all outward appearances seemed doomed. Israel was the apple of God's eye. God had planned this captivity to humble His people, but He already had their deliverance planned in intricate detail.

First, God deals with the proud king Nebuchadnezzar, through the young Israelite, Daniel, and later through the three youths, Shadrach, Meshach, and Abednego, and finally through seven years of madness, when the king ate grass like a cow and grew nails like the claws of eagles. These years of insanity are substantiated by Babylon's own royal records. In those days, the historians were not allowed to record anything derogatory about the king since he was considered divine. The historians, therefore, often used euphemisms to record anything that might be construed as a blot on the king's divine record. In this case, the ancient documents of Babylon read that Nebuchadnezzar was "sick" for seven years. When God removed the insanity from Nebuchadnezzar, the once proud king exclaimed, "Now I Nebuchadnezzar praise and extol and honour the King of heaven, all whose works are truth, and his ways judgment:

and those that walk in pride, he is able to abase" (Dan. 4:37). Nebuchadnezzar was clearly speaking from experience.

Captive Israel faired well under Nebuchadnezzar. Following his death, however, his grandson, Belshazzar became king. Even though Belshazzar had been an eyewitness to the experiences of his grandfather and heard him praise and extol and honor the King of heaven, he still turned away to worship idols.

The final straw came on the night of a great pagan feast Belshazzar had reinstituted. He and a thousand Babylonian leaders were celebrating in the palace when suddenly, Belshazzar remembers those beautiful vessels that his grandfather had brought from the temple of the Israelites. In a deliberate act of sacrilege, Belshazzar orders the vessels brought from the treasure house and "the king, and his princes, his wives, and his concubines, drank in them. They drank wine, and praised the gods of gold, and of silver, of brass, of iron, of wood, and of stone."

As Belshazzar reaches for God's sacred vessel to take another drink, a shadowy movement on the wall suddenly catches his eye. He looks and gasps. There, in the flickering light of a candle, he sees a hand—and the hand is writing on the wall. Belshazzar watches and begins to tremble. Slowly the revelry in the hall dies down as thousands turn to look. Belshazzar's face has turned ashen and his knees shake in fear. Suddenly the hand disappears, but remaining upon the wall are the words, "MENE, MENE, TEKEL, UPHARSIN."

"What does this mean?" Belshazzar screams. "Call the soothsayers! Call the astrologers! Get my wise men in here!"

But none could interpret the strange words.

The queen suddenly remembered Daniel, the young Hebrew who interpreted Nebuchadnezzar's dreams. Belshazzar orders the soldiers to bring Daniel at once.

THE CHRISTIAN EMPLOYEE

Outside, not far from the great walls of Babylon, the Persian army of Cyrus the Great has been camping. They had laid siege to Babylon a few weeks before, but within the security of the walls of Babylon, Belshazzar laughed at Cyrus's futile efforts. Tonight, however, while Belshazzar sits in the luxury of his palace, in a city that has never been equaled in all of history, Cyrus and his men are up to their knees in mud. Tonight, they will try a new strategy.

Meanwhile, escorted by soldiers, Daniel makes his way through the great hall to the king. The hushed crowd falls back to make way for this respected man. Now, he faces the king. Daniel takes one look at the words and knows the meaning.

"O King, you have not humbled your heart as your grandfather did before the true God," Daniel begins, "but you have lifted yourself up against the Lord of heaven and desecrated His holy vessels as you praised the gods of gold and silver. Because of this, God has spoken to you with these words, 'MENE, MENE, TEKEL, UPHARSIN.' This is the meaning of the words. God has numbered your kingdom and finished it. You are weighed in the balances and found wanting. Your kingdom is divided and given to the Medes and the Persians!"

At that very moment, the Persian army of Cyrus the Great was pouring into the city of Babylon. Quickly and quietly, they had dammed up the Euphrates and crawled under the wall—but found themselves enclosed inside the city by the inner walls. Suddenly, a soldier spotted an open gate—then another. Two of the inner gates into the city had been left open. There was not a guard in sight. Cyrus's army slipped through the gates and took the city with little or no resistance.

Within moments, the soldiers burst into the palace hall, captured the drunken princes of Babylon and murdered

Belshazzar. The kingdom of Babylon had fallen to Cyrus the Great.

This is an interesting, dramatic story from the annals of history; but unlike most historical events, it was foretold in detail by God, two hundred years before it happened. It is even more remarkable than most prophecies because of the wealth of details given. In Isaiah 44:27 through 45:4, we find the story of Cyrus the Great and the fall of Babylon:

That saith to the deep, Be dry, and I will dry up thy rivers: That saith of Cyrus, He is my shepherd, and shall perform all my pleasure: even saying to Jerusalem, Thou shalt be built; and to the temple, Thy foundation shall be laid. Thus saith the Lord to his anointed, to Cyrus, whose right hand I have holden, to subdue nations before him; and I will loose the loins of kings, to open before him the two leaved gates; and the gates shall not be shut; I will go before thee, and make the crooked places straight: I will break in pieces the gates of brass, and cut in sunder the bars of iron: And I will give thee the treasures of darkness, and hidden riches of secret places, that thou mayest know that I, the Lord, which call thee by thy name, am the God of Israel. For Jacob my servant's sake, and Israel mine elect, I have even called thee by thy name: I have surnamed thee, though thou hast not known me.

Two hundred years after this was written by the prophet Isaiah, it came to pass with incredible precision. One of the most unusual aspects of this prophecy is that fact that Cyrus is named. God was aware that He was giving more specific information than usual—He emphasized that He was naming names this time! One hundred and fifty years later, in the pagan land of Persia, a couple who had never heard of the Lord God of Israel, much less any document entitled "The Scroll of Isaiah the Prophet," had a son. And they just happened to name him Cyrus. The rest is history.

That saith to the deep be dry, and I will dry up thy rivers. The "deep" referred to the Euphrates and "thy rivers" to the tributaries that "dried up" when Cyrus diverted the flow.

Thus saith the Lord to his anointed, to Cyrus, whose right hand I have holden, to subdue the nations before him. Before Cyrus conquered Babylon, he had defeated, "subdued" thirteen separate nations—the Cilians, Syrians, Maryandines, Sacae, Paphalgonians, Bactrians, Cappdocians, Assyrians, Phygians, Lians, Phoenicians, and the Carians!

I will loose the loins of kings. Remember Belshazzar's reaction when he saw the hand writing on the wall? He began to shake. To "loose the loins" meant to scare someone so badly that their knees shook. Look at this Scripture which describes Belshazzar's reaction: "Then the king's countenance changed, and his thoughts troubled him so that the *joints of his loins were loosed* and his knees smote one against another." Isaiah had foretold Belshazzar's "shaking"; two hundred years later, Daniel recorded the precise fulfillment.

. . . to open before him the two leaved gates, and the gates shall not be shut . . . I will break in pieces the gates of brass and cut in sunder the bars of iron. We have seen that the inner walls had gates, made of *brass* and locked with *iron bars.* We have also seen that when Cyrus and his army crawled under the wall, they should have been trapped—but "the two leaved gates" were open! A prophecy couldn't be more specific than that. God either caused blindness to come upon the guards, or else they were all at the feast, but either way, He opened two gates for Cyrus to enter the city.

I will give thee the treasures of darkness and hidden riches of secret places. By the time Cyrus came against Belshazzar, Babylon had an impressive array of treasures in its national treasury. Grandfather Nebuchadnezzar had been a great military leader (it was he, remember, who captured Israel) and from his conquests the national wealth had swollen to magnificent proportions. After Cyrus conquered Babylon, he took inventory of the treasure house, and historians estimate that the treasures he found were worth approximately $350 million.

As we have seen, Cyrus's most intelligent tactic in conquering Babylon was damming up the river and crawling under the walls. But that tactic—his "best shot"—had already been anticipated. The only reason Cyrus captured Babylon was because God had arranged it. "*I* [God] will dry up thy rivers . . . Cyrus, whose right hand *I* have holden . . . *I* will loose the loins of kings . . . *I* will open before him the two leaved gates . . . *I* will cut in pieces the gates of brass . . . *I* will give thee treasures of darkness. . . ."

Why? Why did God choose to map out the career of one king, Cyrus, and plan his conquest of Babylon with such precision? God gives us the answer in the last phrase of the prophecy. He said, "(I have done all this) . . . that thou mayest know that I, the Lord, which call thee by thy name, am the God of Israel." God wanted Cyrus, a pagan king who lived 2,600 years ago to know that the Lord is God and that He reigns supreme.

God's Building Program

Remember that when Nebuchadnezzar overthrew Israel, he left the temple and the city of Jerusalem in ruins. And now, God, speaking through Isaiah, tells Cyrus "you shall perform *all* my pleasure; you shall rebuild Jerusalem and lay the foundation of the temple." Let's see how Cyrus finds out about his assignment.

When Cyrus took Babylon, he gave the throne to his uncle, Darius the Mede. When Darius later died, Cyrus took personal charge of the city. In the first year of his reign, Cyrus issued a proclamation to all his vast kingdom, and the prophet Ezra recorded it. It read:

> Thus saith Cyrus king of Persia, The Lord God of heaven hath given me all the kingdoms of the earth; and he hath charged me to build him an house at Jerusalem, which is in Judah. Who is there among you of all his people? his God be with him, and let him go up to Jerusalem, which is in Judah, and build the house of the Lord God of Israel, (he is the God,) which is in Jerusalem. (Ezra 1:2-3)

The plot thickens! How did Cyrus know God wanted him to reconstruct the temple in Jerusalem? How is it that a pagan king (and he was still a pagan) could say, "God *told* me to do this. . . ." Why would a king suddenly free a slave nation, tell them to pack up and go home? That was no light thing.

Remember the young man, Daniel, the interpreter of dreams? I suspect he had something to do with Cyrus's proclamation.

Daniel had won favor with Nebuchadnezzar by interpreting his dreams. The king had elevated Daniel to be chief of the princes and ruler of the nation. He continued in high office through the reigns of Belshazzar and Darius. As a privileged person, he also had access to the scrolls of the prophets which were stored in the treasure house along with the sacred objects from the temple in Jerusalem. Thus, studying the scrolls one day (Dan. 9:1-3), Daniel came across the prophecy in Jeremiah concerning the desolation of Israel. The prophecy read in part, "For thus saith the Lord,

That after seventy years be accomplished at Babylon, I will visit you, and perform my good word toward you, in causing you to return to this place" (Jer. 29:10). Israel will be in Babylon for seventy years and then God will deliver His people. Daniel starts counting, and suddenly realizes that Israel has been in Babylon for sixty-nine years! *Only one year left* until God will return His people to their land. So Daniel begins to seek God's face, confessing the sins of Israel and requesting mercy. He prays fervently that God will fulfill His Word.

Shortly after that, Darius died and Cyrus took the throne. Cyrus inherited Daniel as a right-hand man along with the job. Daniel had become an institution by this time. He was the most respected and trusted royal adviser and the only wise man who had any wisdom.

I believe that one day while Daniel was reading in the scroll of Isaiah, he suddenly came across the passage we quoted earlier that mentions Cyrus by name. He realizes that the passage describes the conquest of Babylon. The lights begin to flash in Daniel's mind. "Cyrus . . . is my shepherd," he reads, "and shall perform all my pleasure, even saying to Jerusalem, thou shalt be built, and to the temple, thy foundation. . . ."

"Aha!" Daniel says to himself. "Cyrus is the man. . . ."

What would you do, if you were the right-hand man to the president of a large company and had this kind of information in your possession? You would probably do what Daniel did. He made an appointment for a private discussion with Cyrus.

When the time arrives, Daniel meets Cyrus in the royal office and the two sit down over coffee. Daniel unrolls the scroll of the prophet Isaiah on the table in front of them.

"Sir, I've been doing some research lately, and I've stumbled across some information that will, I believe, be of great interest to you," Daniel begins. He points out to Cyrus the 44th and 45th chapters of Isaiah. "Just read this, sir "

Cyrus takes a sip of coffee and begins to read. He is prepared to read some material pertaining to his kingdom—perhaps a report on the status of the building programs, or a secret document concerning enemy strategy, or a census report by his congressional subcommittee on Internal Affairs and National Assets.

"That saith of Cyrus, he is my shepherd. . . ." Cyrus brings the scroll a little closer and adjusts his glasses. Did he see that correctly? He reads again. There, in print, in this strange, ancient scroll, is his own name. He reads on . . . two leaved gates . . . rivers drying up . . . hidden treasures. He sees before him the conquest of Babylon, detail by detail, just as it happened. He remembers the two gates standing open . . . he remembers each detail of the campaign, and the way Babylon almost fell into his lap.

Cyrus is stunned. Daniel hastens to point out that this scroll is an ancient religious document of the nation of Israel. Perhaps he tells Cyrus about the Lord God of Israel, who parted the sea for His people to cross and gave them bread which appeared on the grass each morning, how their God had given them the land of Judah and defeated their foes for them. . . .

Cyrus reads the passage again. He reaches the last sentence. *"That thou mayest know,* Cyrus, that I, the Lord, which called thee by name, am the God of Israel."

"This book, sir, was written two hundred years ago, one hundred and fifty years before you were born," Daniel repeats. But Cyrus is already convinced. This God of Israel isn't just another god made by hands. He looks up at Daniel and exclaims, "He *is* God."

After Cyrus recovers from the shock, he reads that God wants him to "say to Jerusalem, be built, and to the temple, thy foundation shall be laid." Cyrus immediately issues that proclamation, sending the Israelites back home. He also ordered that gifts be given to the house of God. ". . . let the men of his place [the neighbors of the Hebrews] help him with silver, and with gold, and with goods, and with beasts, beside the freewill offering for the house of God that is in Jerusalem" (Ezra 1:4). In addition, the kings who succeeded Cyrus honored the decree with financial support, and in time Babylon returned all the holy vessels and other sacred objects to Israel.

The Israelites, laden with gifts of jewelry, oxen, food, and other goods, set out for home, after seventy years of being slaves. All that God had wanted done, was done.

The King of Kings

We are accustomed to thinking that God is concerned only with Christians. We feel that somehow God doesn't—or, even, can't—exercise as much control over the rest of the world as He does over Christians and Christian affairs.

Yet how many times do we call Jesus the King of kings and the Lord of lords? That title which the Father has given to His Son means that Jesus is the King over all the kings of the earth and Lord over all the lords (masters) of the earth. Christ is not just *over* them in some remote heavenly hierarchy, but over them in authority and control here and now.

The ultimate example of God's control over men, regardless of their beliefs, is the crucifixion itself. When Jesus hung on the cross, it appeared that God had lost control of the situation—it seemed to the dsiciples that the course of events had gotten out of hand and gone too far.

But God had engineered the whole event. He had planned the crucifixion even down to the smallest details—the spear thrust in His side; the unbroken bones; even His words, "My

God, my God, why hast thou forsaken me?" All these details had been foretold in prophecy in the Old Testament. Many details of the crucifixion were departures from the normal procedure for this method of execution. The guards usually broke the legs of the criminal who was being crucified; they didn't normally spear the criminal in the side; and many other unusual details were involved in this crucifixion. In warning His disciples of His crucifixion, Jesus told them, "No man *taketh* my life from me, but *I lay it down of myself.*" Over and over, He revealed that He and the Father were in control of the situation every step of the way.

God is not just "up there" vaguely supervising. He is not in control of the generalities, overall trends and big events only, but is also in charge of each step and each detail. As children, we sang the song, "He's Got the Whole World in His Hands"; it's truer than we thought! He does have the *whole world*—the people, the politics, the kings, the governments, the congressional votes, the summit meetings and the labor unions—in His hands.

We often hear the expressions, "he got a lucky break," or "he just happened to be in the right place at the right time," or "that sure was a freak accident." People who want to wish someone well almost invariably say "Good luck!" Most non-Christians view themselves as being at the mercy of some impersonal force called chance or fate or luck. But what a different picture of the world the Word of God paints for us. ". . . God . . . is the blessed controller of all things" (1 Tim. 6:15, Phillips). According to God, there is neither fate nor accident, but only the intricate plan gradually unfolding with everything that happens in our lives. The same God who was so specifically involved in the life of Cyrus the Great is today involved—and to the same extent—in the lives of politicians, scientists, corporate presidents and in *your* life.

Since I first experienced first-hand the power and control

of God over the world—the secular world—my attitude toward work has never been the same. I saw that God was God over events that were not religious and over people who were not Christian.

While I was working for the federal government, I was given an assignment in a foreign country. The United States and this country had agreed to jointly finance a major construction project. My particular assignment involved selecting a qualified consultant firm to do some preliminary engineering work on the project.

The representatives of this foreign government and our government had already compiled a list of firms as candidates for this job. Now the final selection had to be made and I was sent to that country to meet with the officials to assist in making the final decision. Before I left, however, my superiors filled me in on the details of the previous meetings and gave me some of the behind-the-scenes information. One of the firms that was in the front running for selection was politically active; it had certain connections with the local government officials who were trying to advance the firm for their own purposes of exploitation. Kickbacks and payoffs were a way of life in this particular country and the officials with whom I would work could very well be involved.

There was another firm which was also strong in the running—and we knew it to be an ethical and competent company. My superiors told me, "Do all that you can to influence the decision in favor of Company A (the ethical firm). If Company B gets the job, a considerable sum of money will be wasted on kickbacks and poor engineering work. . . ."

I flew to the country on a weekend and the meetings with the government officials began Monday morning. As I went into the meetings I knew this situation must be handled diplomatically; I must not say anything that suggested Company B was dishonest or corrupt. Throughout the day we presented arguments for and against each company but at the end of the meeting late that afternoon, no real progress had been made.

The meetings continued two, three, then four days. Each day we spent thirty minutes telling each other where we had had dinner the night before, what we had eaten, and whether or not the meal was good. We caught up on local news, the new plant that opened last week, the new restaurant that would open next week, and the band concert tonight. But when the coffee was served, the congenial conversation ended abruptly and we turned to the matter at hand. Each day was the same—the same arguments, the same opinions. We were in a deadlock.

For every logical argument I offered, the officials offered another equally logical one in rebuttal. It became clear to me that as long as we skirted the real issue—honesty and competency—no progress could be made. The officials weren't about to assign a project of this magnitude to a competitor of Company B; they couldn't "forget their pocketbooks" and I couldn't "look the other way." And since I could not bring the real issue out into the open, we went around and around on the secondary, technical points. There was simply no way we could agree on a firm.

At the end of the meeting on Thursday night, I went back to my motel room discouraged and confused. There was nothing else I could say to convince the officials. I had presented every argument I could devise, yet they remained adamantly in favor of Company B. In the quietness of my room, I began to pray, "Lord, I don't understand what's going on. As best I know how, I'm doing my part. I'm being obedient to my superiors' instructions and to my conscience—but the situation is still hopeless. What should I do?" I asked God whether I should give in or confront the officials with the issue of honesty. I prayed earnestly for His wisdom.

When no answer came, I went out to get dinner, more discouraged than ever. After I returned to my room and got ready for bed, I picked up a book I had brought on the trip with me. I had been reading it for about five minutes, when suddenly a Scripture quoted in the book jumped off the page at me. "Remember ye not the former things, neither consider the things of old. Behold, I will do a new thing; now it shall spring forth; shall ye not know it? I will even make a way in the wilderness . . ." (Isa. 43:18-19).

Through those words, God spoke to me, giving me the answer to my dilemma. He was telling me to forget the things that had passed, all the failures of the past week, because He was going to do something new. He was going to make a path for me through the wilderness I was in. I jumped up out of bed and began walking around the room, praising God. His presence seemed to fill the whole room.

The next morning at breakfast, I decided that I would not even offer any more arguments. I had a sense of excitement and anticipation—God had said that He would do a new thing and I knew He didn't need my help.

The meeting began with the usual pleasantries. When the coffee was served, we took our places at the conference table to begin discussions once more. The Minister of Public Works, the official who would make the final decision, took a sip of coffee very slowly, set his cup down, and looked around the table at the men, carefully studying each face. I was getting more excited by the moment.

"Gentlemen," he began, "I stayed up quite late last night, thinking about this situation. I have changed my mind. We will hire Company A to do work on this project. That is my decision."

THE CHRISTIAN EMPLOYEE

He spoke on, giving instructions on drawing up the contract, but I never heard another word. I sat stunned; everything around me seemed to fade away and the voices seemed distant. The meeting adjourned in a few minutes and everyone filed out. As the room emptied, I stood alone by the window and looked out over the city. I felt at that moment as though God put His arm around me and said, "Son, I just wanted you to know; I am God and there is no other beside me." Tears came to my eyes.

I remembered the many times the Scriptures say that God spoke to a king or a leader, waking them up in the middle of the night sometimes, to direct their decisions. I saw how easily God had accomplished what four days of lengthy discussions could not—convincing the minister to change his mind.

To my knowledge, none of the officials involved in the meetings were Christians, but that fact had no bearing on the fulfillment of God's will. Individuals and nations fulfill God's purposes every day all over the world without even realizing it. Cyrus never knew God while he was conquering fourteen nations or when he crawled under the wall of Babylon.

If God can rule nations and direct the course of events all over the world in every area of life, is it possible that He can rule and direct your office? If He can control all the Cyruses and all the ministers of public works, does He have the ability to control your place of work? If He is able to change the direction of a construction project, can He not direct businesses in any area, as you go about your daily job?

The Word of God says that ". . . the most high God ruled in the kingdom of men, and that he appointeth over it whomsoever he will" (Dan. 5:21).

The first of seven principles of employment and the one which lays the foundation for all the rest is:

GOD CONTROLS KINGDOMS AND COMPANIES

CHAPTER FIVE

Promotion Cometh neither from the East nor the West

Another serious symptom of the MMM Syndrome is severe spiritual myopia—extreme nearsightedness. We see the boss, the man set immediately over us, as looming paramount in our careers. He, we think, is the one who has the power over us. He is the one who holds the future in his hands. He is the one who holds the reins of our careers. And because we cannot see *beyond* him, he is the one we try to please. We want to earn his respect—the respect that results in raises and promotions. Either consciously or subconsciously, we try to secure our positions and ward off his displeasure. We solicit his favor by being nice to him, at least to his face. We compliment him on his family, his good judgment, his good taste in neckties. But at heart, we are tired of the strain and worry, and the effort of trying to manipulate ourselves and others.

In addition to our natural tendencies to please the boss for selfish motives, many companies have designed fail-safe systems that are deliberately used to keep employees hopping. Policies that promote competition, all in the name of "keeping them on their toes," actually encourage suspicion, job insecurity, and disloyalty in an office. But some employers still insist that working in an atmosphere of fear keeps employees alert.

William Randolph Hearst, the famous newspaper mogul, often used a practice he learned from his arch rival, Joseph Pulitzer, of hiring two men for the same job and letting them fight it out. The one who came out on top, either by superior skill or a scheme to make his foe look bad, was given the job.

Less extreme company policies include setting quotas to establish performance standards, conducting intra-company contests for money or a trip to Hawaii, and other incentive devices, that invariably put employees in direct competition with each other. And almost all companies have annual performance ratings in which each employee is graded on everything from the quality of his work to his personal appearance. The effect is to keep the employees wondering what the boss thinks about not only his work but his manners and choice of shirts. Some companies today are even using computers to rate the employees' work, potential and even future output.

But we have seen that God controls kingdoms and companies. So, how does knowing this truth help us to face the nitty-gritty world of competition, advancement, salary, and the ever-present possibility of being fired or laid off because of some distant event on Wall Street, in Detroit, or in Saudi Arabia?

If we can believe that God controls the company, then our next principle of employment follows naturally:

YOUR ENTIRE FUTURE IS DETERMINED BY GOD AND YOUR RESPONSE TO HIM—NOT BY YOUR COMPANY

God promises us rewards repeatedly in the Scriptures. But rewards are dependent upon two factors: (1) God's plan for our lives and (2) our response to God as the plan unfolds. God and our response to Him will determine an upward or downward course for our careers and our lives. Instead of trying to please the boss, we should turn our attention to pleasing God. Our failure to do this is a measure of our unbelief. So, let's confess our unbelief, get cleansed, and try again. We must transfer the power we have assigned to the boss to God instead.

When you fully comprehend that God and your response to Him determine your career, you will be set free from worry You will no longer fret about achievement. You will no longer worry about the boss's opinion of you. You will not get ulcers over meeting quotas or performance ratings. *None of these things have any bearing whatsoever on your future.* You can produce the worst performance rating in the history of your company and still be promoted to general manager; you can produce the best rating ever and still be fired.

"Many seek the ruler's favour; but every man's judgment cometh from the Lord" (Prov. 29:26). No matter how hard we try to win the boss's approval, God is the one who passes judgment on our work. An even stronger Scripture is: "Promotion cometh neither from the east, nor from the west, nor from the south. But God is the judge: he putteth down one, and setteth up another" (Ps. 75:6-7).

To Eat or Not to Eat?

Remember the young lad, Daniel, who was taken captive to Babylon with the nation of Israel? If anyone lacked a future, it was him, a poor slave boy in a foreign land. Daniel should, by natural standards, have remained a poor slave boy, but he didn't, because he had the only asset that matters—God was with Daniel. God had a plan for Daniel's life and He was pleased by Daniel's response to Him as the plan was put into effect.

When the captive Israelites arrived in Babylon, Nebuchadnezzar gave orders to the department of education to search among the newcomers for the brightest minds and talents. The children of this new people were examined, given achievement tests, and interviewed, to select the most promising "in whom there was no blemish." In addition to being intelligent and without physical deformity, the children, according to the Scriptures, had also to be popular with the people of Israel.

The children were taken from their families and assigned to live at the king's palace, where they would be not only educated, but also pampered. They would eat at the king's table, where they would be served the richest, most elaborate of the king's food and served the finest of the king's wine. Among the children of Israel selected for this program were four young boys named Daniel, Shadrach, Meshach, and Abednego.

No sooner had the boys arrived at the palace than a conflict arose. When they appeared at dinner that first night, Daniel took one look at the food and said to himself, "Uh-oh—I can't eat this!" The Scriptures tell us that the boy "purposed in his heart that he would not defile himself with the portion of the king's meat" (Dan. 1:8).

Can you imagine being selected for a scholarship, an honor that would assure you an exalted career; then being invited to live in the palace of the most famous king in the world; then having the biggest feast a boy ever laid eyes on set down in front of you—and then complaining about the food?

But something was seriously wrong with the meat. It may have been meat of a forbidden animal such as a swine; or it may have been improperly butchered, or it may have been from an animal that had been dedicated to idols in pagan sacrifice. Any of these would have violated the Mosaic law. Daniel, raised in a kosher home as a devout believer, knew that he could not eat the meat without breaking God's law.

Daniel slips from the table and finds the eunuch who had been assigned as the directing supervisor of the children, a man with whom Daniel had already found favor.

"Sir," he whispers to the eunuch, "I can't eat this meat. . . ."

"But you must!" the eunuch answers emphatically. "If you don't eat the meat, you will become skinny and pale and the king will cut off my head for letting you get in that condition. He'll cut your head off too for refusing to eat properly! And don't you know meat is part of a healthy diet? No, lad, I'm sorry, but you *have* to eat that meat."

Now let's analyze this situation for a moment, because Daniel's solution to this predicament is of vast significance for us today. He, a mere boy with no security in this pagan land, has inadvertently been ordered to commit a sin against God. In the secular work world, our superiors may also ask us to violate God's law It might be only a matter of a little white lie, a little dishonesty, a little business practice that isn't quite wrong, but not quite right either, depending upon how you look at it. If we refuse, our positions are threatened and, perhaps, the boss's position, too.

Before we examine what Daniel did, let's look at what he *didn't* do. He did not get angry, defensive, and pious. Without self-righteousness, he realized that the eunuch also had a serious problem; he had to keep the Hebrew children healthy. Daniel saw the problem from the eunuch's perspective.

"I tell you what," Daniel said to the eunuch after a thoughtful moment, "let's try an experiment. Permit my friends and me to eat only vegetables for ten days, while the others eat the king's meat. Then at the end of ten days, examine us and compare us with the others, and if we don't look as good, or even better than the others, then deal with us as you see fit."

"That's fair enough," the eunuch agreed. "We'll try it."

The eunuch judged the four boys at the end of ten days and found them "fairer and fatter" than all the others who ate the king's meat. From then on, the eunuch allowed the four boys to eat their own food.

Daniel's solution to this difficult situation rivals, in my opinion, all the wisdom of Solomon. He devised what Bill Gothard calls a *creative alternative*, and its importance for us cannot be overemphasized. The eunuch's viewpoint was "You must eat or we'll both lose our heads." That was all the eunuch could see. Daniel, on the other hand, was not afflicted with myopia and said, "I tell you what, let's try. . . ."

As Daniel stood there pondering the situation, God gave him the wisdom and creativity to see a way out. When your boss gives you an order that requires you to violate God's principles, God will also provide wisdom for you, if you ask. He will help you see a creative alternative, through which He will be glorified.

But if you fly off the handle and say, "Me? Never! I'm a Christian," you will have effectively tied God's hands in that situation. And if you have jeopardized another person's position by your righteousness, you have not been righteous at all, only selfish. A God-given creative alternative will result in a peaceable solution which gains freedom for you in your work and also gains you the boss's respect.

And the beauty of a creative alternative is that it does not make you compromise God's law. Daniel didn't say, "If we don't look as good as the others, then we'll eat the king's meat." He said, "If we don't look as good as the others, then *deal with us as you see fit."*

A creative alternative can turn those difficult situations involving ethics into opportunities for you. Try using a creative alternative the next time you are faced with a request to do something which involves violating God's principles. But remember to:

1) *Respect your superior's position and authority:* Daniel respected the eunuch's position of authority over the Hebrew children. That gave Daniel *two* responsibilities: he could not violate God's law, and he could not jeopardize his boss's position, in this case, his very life.

2) *Recognize your superior's limited frame of reference:* Daniel knew God; the eunuch did not. That gave Daniel both an advantage and a responsibility. He had unlimited power and wisdom at his disposal. The eunuch, on the other hand, was concerned only with losing his head. The boss is concerned only with the success of the company and his own future security. He doesn't want to lose his job when he's forty-seven years old and would lose his pension. His response, like the eunuch's, will be "you *must* do it or we'll both be fired." *You* must take the initiative, realizing that God wants *you* to be the instrument of His wisdom and peace.

3) *Present a reasonable request which does not challenge the superior's authority or force the issue:* Daniel presented a reasonable suggestion. He didn't suggest that all the children refuse the king's meat. He didn't suggest that he and the eunuch go to the king and debate the validity of God's law versus the validity of the king's diet. Furthermore, Daniel didn't challenge the eunuch's authority. He didn't say, "How in the world did *you* get this job, when you don't know anything about Mosaic law?" Daniel, in fact, deferred to the eunuch, saying, "I recognize your position and responsibility and I appreciate it. *You*

make the decision, *you* judge us at the end of ten days. I put the whole matter in *your* hands."

4) *Suggest a reasonable deadline for resolution of the problem:* Daniel suggested ten days, not two months or a year. And, by being specific, you exercise faith and thus give God a chance to act in a way that will bring glory to Him. Daniel simply backed away and allowed God to move to the fore. And look at what God did: He so increased those vegetables in nutrients and calories that the four boys actually got *fat* from them. If you try to force your superior to make a decision that moment, you can be sure he will decide in *his* favor. He will say, "You must do this." Then, God has to either let you lose your job, and lose your patch of people you're supposed to be harvesting, or else God has to strike the superior dead to keep your job secure. God's way is the peaceable way and the way that glorifies Him.

God had tested Daniel. The significance of the incident was not so much the meat itself, as it was the spirit of obedience manifested by Daniel and his three friends. God blessed the four boys for their faithfulness to one small point of the Mosaic law, because they were actually being faithful to Him. What was the blessing? At the end of the three-year training period conducted by Neb's department of education, all the children were brought before the king for the final exam. And "in all matters of wisdom and understanding, that the king enquired of them, he found them ten times better than all the magicians and astrologers that were in all his realm" (Dan. 1:20).

What about the other Hebrew children who ate the king's meat and drank the king's wine? What happened to them? Nothing. But that's just the point. God didn't punish them for eating the meat, but neither did He bless them and use them. While Daniel, Shadrach, Meshach, and Abednego would serve as ruling princes of the nations and have their famous adventures in faith with God, we hear nothing about the other Hebrew children. They simply lived and died in Babylon. Through these faithful four, however, the kings of Babylon saw the power of the God of Israel.

Jesus spoke of the importance of faithfulness in small tasks in the parable of the talents. When the first servant reported to the master what he had done with his talents, the master said, "Well done, thou good and faithful servant. *Thou hast been faithful over a few things. I will make thee ruler over many.*" Daniel and his friends were faithful in a few things and God made them rulers over many

All of God's Word is true and timeless. Is it possible, therefore, that many Christians do not advance in their positions of employment today because they simply are not faithful in a small matter, over a few things? We watch our superiors and think, "If I had his job, I could really get this company moving." We picture ourselves as executive dynamos, expanding the company operations internationally in scope and putting the company on a firm financial basis.

But while we dwell on what the boss isn't doing that we *could* do, we aren't doing what we *should* do. We neglect the work that is right before us, because it doesn't seem important or interesting. We have too high opinions of our own worth.

Only when we humble ourselves to perform every task God sets before us, will He elevate us. God does not intend for His children to drag behind the world in achievement and status. God's children should always be ahead of the world, not because we drive to fulfill ambitions, but because God empowers us with ability and then advances us when we *use* that ability properly.

"Promotion cometh neither from the east, nor from the west, nor from the south. But God is the judge: he putteth down one, and setteth up another." Your future, your career, depends entirely upon God and your response to Him.

His Ways Work

Tom, a new Christian, had an opportunity to test the validity of God's creative alternatives on the job. When Tom came to the Lord, he immediately began witnessing to everyone at work—*everyone*. God began to move and it wasn't long before several co-workers and secretaries were born again and filled with the Holy Spirit. And *they* began to witness.

Earl, Tom's boss, had gradually grown concerned about this. Several times a week, he noticed members of his staff deep in conversation over an open Bible. At first he thought the excitement would die down and the witnessing would cool off, but as months passed the witnessing continued and even spread, as more people came to the Lord. As the witnessing spread, so did Earl's concern over what *his* boss would think if he dropped by the office and saw all the Bible study going on.

The day came when Earl felt he had to say something to Tom about this situation. As Tom came into his office, Earl shut the door behind him and motioned for him to sit down.

"Tom," Earl began cautiously, "I've been meaning to talk to you for some time now about this witnessing. It's got to stop. I've waited for a long time to see if perhaps the situation would stop on its own, but it hasn't. I'm sorry, Tom."

He continued to explain his position. "I am a Christian also and I believe in witnessing to others, but not on company time." What a man does before eight o'clock and after five is his own business, he said, but those hours in between belong to the company.

Tom had listened carefully to the boss's words, praying all

the while. When Earl finished, Tom had a suggestion.

"Sir, have any of the people who are witnessing failed in any part of their work?" he asked. "Are any of them behind schedule?"

"Why no," Earl said thoughtfully, "no one. . . ."

"Then may I suggest something?" Tom continued. "If one of us fails in any tasks, or falls behind schedule at any time, then we will all stop witnessing. But as long as no one neglects his duties in any way, may we continue?"

Earl thought for a moment.

"That's fair," he decided. "It's a deal."

Tom, like Daniel, could have gotten hot over the situation. He could have said, "Jesus told us to preach the gospel and I'm going to do it! You'll have to fire me before I stop preaching!" And Earl would have fired him, not over the witnessing, but over his attitude and defiance, and that would have put a sure end to the witnessing. Because Tom allowed God to move in behalf of the gospel, the witnessing in that office is still going on today after many years.

Over the years, no one has neglected any phase of his or her job.

But If Not. . . .

What happens when a creative alternative is not possible, because your boss will not agree to a reasonable suggestion?

We need to examine this question, because if promotion truly comes ultimately from God alone, *it should not matter whether your boss goes along with your creative alternative or not.* If God alone promotes you, then your boss's opinion should not make any difference, right?

The eunuch already liked Daniel before the meat problem arose. Earl already liked Tom and was already a witnessing Christian. What would have happened if the eunuch and Earl were furious and determined *not* to agree to any solution?

Let's see if, indeed, it would make a difference.

One night King Nebuchadnezzar has a dream that really troubles him. When he takes his seat on the throne the next morning to begin the day's business, he calls for all the astrologers and the magicians. When they arrive, he orders them to interpret his dream.

"Tell us," they request, "what you dreamed, O king, and we will tell you the meaning of it."

"Oh, no," the king answers testily. "If you really have any powers, *you* will tell *me* the dream *and* the interpretation!"

Their answer is most interesting.

"We cannot do anything like that!" they insist. "No flesh, no human being can do anything like *that*. Only the gods can do what you are asking. . . ." Then they made their mistake. They exclaimed, "*And God does not dwell with flesh!*"

That makes the king livid with rage. If the gods do not dwell in men, then why does he have all these magicians and astrologers on the payroll? He is *paying* them to have "gods dwell with flesh" and now they can't deliver the goods. Enraged, the king sends out a decree to have all the worthless fellows executed.

The soldiers begin rounding everyone up who is a wise man, soothsayer, magician, seer, or astrologer. Finally, one big, burly soldier arrives at Daniel's door. Daniel is the most famous wise man of them all. When Daniel answers the door, the soldier says politely, "Please come with me. I've been ordered to chop off your head. Sorry, king's orders." Daniel convinces the soldier to at least let him see the king first.

When Daniel appears before the king, he respectfully asks why he is going to be beheaded. The king explains to Daniel that all the court wise men are frauds.

"None of you have any power!" the king screams. "None of you can do anything! You just take my gold and do nothing in return. I had a dream and no one could tell me the meaning! They say 'O king, God doesn't dwell with flesh!' The very idea!"

Daniel answers, again with a creative alternative.

"King, since you are going to kill me anyway, why don't you give me a chance to seek God for the interpretation of your dream," he offers. "I wasn't with your court wise men this morning, so I haven't had a chance. If I can't give you a description of your dream and then tell you the meaning by morning, then kill me."

Neb sees that he has nothing to lose and everything to gain, so he agrees.

Daniel hotfoots it back to the office and calls his three closest colleagues, Shadrach, Meshach, and Abednego. "Come on, boys, we've got to pray!"

That night, Daniel awakes from his sleep, suddenly realizing that he has had a dream. God has given him the king's dream! As he prays further, God unfolds the meaning to him. The next morning, as *early* as possible, Daniel runs to the palace to see the king.

"O king, this is what you dreamed," Daniel exclaims. "You saw a giant image of a man. The head of the image was gold. . ." and he goes on to describe in precise detail that the breast of the image was silver; the thighs were brass; the legs were iron; the feet were iron and clay mixed. Neb is all smiles—and all ears.

"Now, O king, this is what it means," Daniel continues. "The four parts of the image stand for four kingdoms. You are the head of gold; the breast of silver is the kingdom of . . ." and he tells what each kingdom is, the outcome of each kingdom.

But Neb didn't hear another word. He got hung up on the head of gold and didn't hear another word Daniel said. "The head of gold—that's *me!* the head of gold—*I'm* the head of gold! By George, I like this fellow!"

Daniel's life is saved, and Neb is thoroughly pleased. Here is a wise man with *real* power, and a man who says such nice things about his majesty. Before long, we find Neb building himself a giant image, of himself, of course, and of *solid gold*. He doesn't bother with accuracy—this image doesn't have a breast of silver or thighs of brass. It is solid gold from the top of its magnificent head to the bottom of its gilded feet.

When the image was finished by the craftsmen of Babylon, the king ordered it hauled to the center of the city for all to see. Now, it looms over the Babylon city square, glistening radiantly in the sun. Neb likes it so well. It's grand enough to worship.

That called for a decree. The court wise men think it's a splendid idea. It's been awfully boring around here since those Hebrews came—but now, some fun! The decree ordered that when Neb motioned for the royal orchestra to play, all the people upon hearing the music were to stop their work, come out of their houses and shops, and bow to the ground at the feet of the golden image of the king.

The time for the first worship service arrived. Neb signals for the music to begin and all the people rush to the feet of the image and bow themselves low. Neb was *so* pleased.

The only problem is that when everyone else bows, and you don't, you're very *conspicuous*. In the vast crowd of figures bowed to the ground, there were three lone men still standing. And there will always be someone around to notice when you don't bow to images; there will always be some who will be happy to inform on you! There will always be a Chaldean in the next office who sees you standing tall in a sea of bowed figures.

The Chaldeans were just delighted to inform the king of the three men who wouldn't bow. The men were, of course, Shadrach, Meshach, and Abednego.

"King, your majesty and glorious highness! We saw someone refuse to bow down to your beautiful image!" they report breathlessly, with the same enthusiasm of a little boy who has been *waiting* to tell on his brother. "We saw them with our own eyes—those three men over there—those three Hebrews!"

Neb orders the three men brought to him at once.

"What is this I hear?" he cries. "Is it possible that you refused to bow to my image?" he asked incredulously. "I'm going to play the music once more and if you don't bow down this time, I'll throw you into the fiery furnace!" Then he asks what he thinks is merely a rhetorical question.

"And who is that God that shall deliver you out of my hands?" He was not asking them to tell him about their God. Instead, he was really saying, "there is *no* God that can deliver you."

I don't believe that Shadrach, Meshach, and Abednego were feeling very spiritual at that moment. I believe they were probably frightened. There was nothing they could say to quench this man's anger. Neb was determined to make them worship the image, and thereby worship *him*, and no answer the three men could give would be enough. There was absolutely no room for a creative alternative. Look at their answer to the king. It is an amazing statement of faith.

"O Nebuchadnezzar, we are not careful to answer thee in this matter. If it be so, our God whom we serve is able to deliver us from the burning fiery furnace, and He will deliver us out of thine hand, O king. *But if not, be it known unto thee, O king, that we will not serve thy gods, nor worship the golden image which thou hast set up.*"

Their answer only makes Neb madder. He orders the furnace heated seven times hotter than usual and orders the three men bound tightly. The furnace became so hot that the heat *outside* the furnace was intense enough to kill the three guards who threw the Hebrews into the furnace.

Naturally, they should have died instantly. As soon as the doors are closed, Neb sits down comfortably, thinking, "Well, I guess their god chose *not* to deliver them—ha ha!"

As Neb comes as close to the furnace as he dares, straining to see through the flames, he suddenly wheels around to a guard.

"Didn't we throw three men, with their hands and legs bound, into the furnace?"

"Yes, O king," the guard assures him. "There were three men—the three Hebrews."

"Then why do I see four men—and they're walking around, unbound, in the midst of the flames! And the form of the fourth is like unto the Son of God!"

Neb, shaking from head to toe, orders the men brought out immediately. The men walk to the furnace door, step out, but now there are only three men again.

Neb, the great king of Babylon, stares at them. Not only were they unharmed, but their clothes were unsinged and had not even the smell of fire.

"There is no other God that can deliver after this manner," Neb announces.

He immediately issues a decree that everyone in the kingdom shall henceforth bow down to the God of Shadrach, Meshach, and Abednego, with dire results for anyone who refuses. At last, the worship that Neb demanded for himself is given to the God who can deliver.

In this situation, Shadrach, Meshach, and Abednego had no opportunity to present a creative alternative. Neb wanted nothing less than their worship, which they could not give. They gave the only answer they could give a man who thought he was worthy of worship: "The true God is able to deliver us, but if not, we still will not worship you." There was no middle ground; no ten-day trial period. God had to intervene at that moment or His faithful servants would burn to ashes.

You may occasionally face a situation when your circumstances could be classified as a genuine emergency. It is important for us to see that God doesn't fail, whether we have seconds, minutes, hours, or days to be rescued. It is also important for us to see that God's power isn't dependent upon our spirituality. Throughout their lives, the three men had looked to Daniel for guidance and advice. But this time Daniel was not involved. God will put us in situations when our spiritual mentor, the man or woman who has provided the insight and wisdom to see solutions, is not there. It comes down to a matter of "it's just you and me, Lord." He will never fail.

Let's look at another situation involving immediate danger, similar to the one Shadrach, Meshach, and Abednego faced.

When Darius became king of Babylon, years after Nebuchadnezzar's death, he chose 120 princes to rule the kingdom. Over these, he chose three presidents, of which Daniel was the chief. Daniel "was preferred above the presidents and princes because an excellent spirit was in him" (Dan. 6:3).

Remember the Chaldeans who reported Shadrach, Meshach, and Abednego to the king? Well, Daniel also had some Chaldeans in the office next door, and they were out to get him. Any time God brings you into favor with the boss, there are going to be Chaldeans watching you every minute. The Bible records that these men, probably jealous of Daniel, started plotting against him. They just waited for him to make a mistake to pounce on him. Finally they concluded, "We shall not find any occasion against this Daniel *except we find it against him concerning the law of his God.*" There was no fault in Daniel. The only way they could destroy him was by trapping him in a matter of God's laws. So they devised a scheme.

"King Darius," they began as they presented themselves to the king, "we just came up with a wonderful idea. We think you should send out a decree that no man in the kingdom is permitted to ask anything of their god or of any man for a period of thirty days unless they come to you first. This will show the kingdom how wise and powerful you are!"

"I really like that," Darius said. "That's a great idea. Draft the decree and I'll sign it today."

The only problem was that the law of the Medes and Persians allowed no change or modification in a decree until it had run its course. Even the king could not rescind the decree; and the punishment for breaking the law was execution by lions.

Picture Daniel in his office when the decree arrives. He receives this memorandum, reads it carefully, and then files it in the waste basket. At the usual time of prayer and worship, Daniel tells his secretary that he is going home for the day. When he arrives at home, he opens the patio doors, gets right out in the open, as he always does, faces west toward Jerusalem, bows down before the Lord and prays.

Guess who's looking over the back fence? The Chaldeans, of course. They hotfoot it to the palace, wringing their hands in glee, and rejoicing over their good fortune.

"King! You know that decree you sent out this morning? Well, we caught a man violating it right out in the open, deliberately defying you!" they exclaim.

Darius orders the Chaldeans to bring the man to him immediately.

"Here's the offender!" the Chaldeans announce. "You know the law—he must be put to death!" Darius was appalled to see Daniel standing before him in custody.

The Scriptures read, "Then the king, when he heard these

words, was sore displeased with himself, and set his heart on Daniel to deliver him: and he laboured till the going down of the sun to deliver him."

Darius loved Daniel. He knew that God was with this Hebrew and he loved him for his "excellent spirit." When he saw that he had allowed these base Chaldeans to trap him in his own ego to destroy a friend he loved, he was angry with himself and worked all afternoon trying to find a loophole to get Daniel out of the death penalty.

But every argument Darius devised was refused by the court legal experts. How could order be maintained, they insisted, if the king would not obey his own law. And, if Darius broke the law, think of the repercussions throughout the empire, they warned.

Darius calls for Daniel to break the bad news.

"Thy God, whom thou servest continually, he will deliver thee," Darius said sadly. That was his last hope.

The Chaldeans took Daniel to the lions' den and cast him in. A great stone was rolled in front of the entrance and Darius sealed it with his own royal signet. That way the king couldn't send guards later to rescue his beloved friend.

Then, "the king went to his palace and passed the night fasting." He still didn't give up. Darius fasted *for* his friend and *to* the God of his friend.

The next morning, the king arose very early and rushed to the lions' den, and "cried with a lamentable voice . . . O Daniel, servant of the living God, is thy God, whom thou servest continually, able to deliver thee from the lions?" Imagine the pain this man was suffering at that moment.

But immediately he hears his friend's voice.

"My God hath sent his angel, and hath shut the lions' mouths, that they have not hurt me: forasmuch as before him innocency was found in me; and also before thee, O king, have I done no hurt."

THE CHRISTIAN EMPLOYEE

Then Darius was exceedingly glad and commanded the Chaldeans to bring Daniel out of the den. When Daniel was brought out, the Chaldeans were cast *in*, by Darius's order, and devoured immediately by the lions.

We have examined two cases of God's power to deliver—once from a fiery furnace and another from the lions' den. Both stories illustrate God's power to deliver.

But the two stories are different in one important respect. In the first case, we saw an enraged king who declared, *"Who is that god who is able to deliver thee out of my hand?"* In the second case, we saw a troubled king who said, *"Thy God, whom thou servest continually, he is able to deliver thee."* The attitudes were opposite, but *the outcome was the same.*

Neb *hated* Shadrach, Meshach, and Abednego; but Darius *loved* Daniel. God delivered them *both*. Could Neb's hatred render God's power of no avail? No. Could Darius's love deliver Daniel? No.

What does this mean? It means that *it makes no difference how your boss feels about you.* He can hate you, and God will deliver. He can love you, and God will still deliver. The results are the same.

The only thing that has any bearing on your career is your relationship with God. If you are right in your heart with God, He will deliver you from the fiery furnace. And when you come out, you won't even have the smell of smoke on your clothes. God will deliver you from the mouths of lions. He will walk with you in the midst of hungry lions and you will not be devoured. The lions will strangely lose their appetites for you.

In both cases, the "victims" were innocent. In answering Darius, Daniel said, "I am not hurt, *because* innocency was found in me." He was referring to his relationship with God. The *only* reason he was delivered from the lions was because he was right in his heart with God.

Your boss's attitude toward you doesn't matter, but God's attitude toward you *does* matter. It is the *only* thing that matters.

Your future is determined by God and your response to Him alone.

CHAPTER SIX

Accident or Engineered?

What about those times when things didn't turn out so well, when you stood on your faith in God and disaster still struck? What about that time you were passed over for a promotion and the man who got the job was much less competent than you—and you *had* been faithful over the little things? Or what about the time you were blamed for missing an important deadline, when it was, in reality, Jim's fault?

In the face of adverse circumstances, we normally become depressed, either mildly or severely. And depression, as we have seen, is a very real *symptom* of the Monday Morning Mulligrubs Syndrome.

We have seen from the life of Daniel that God is responsible for our rewards and promotions. But we have not examined the role He plays in our failures. When the worst happens, is it God's fault, or our fault, or maybe Satan's fault? Is God punishing us? Are we reaping what we sowed—somehow? What went wrong?

God gives us the answer to this age-old debate in the life story of Joseph. By His involvement in Joseph's life, God reveals exactly what role He plays in adverse circumstances.

Behold, This Dreamer

The boy Joseph had an interesting dream, and, one day while he was out in the fields of his father's farm, in his youthful enthusiasm (he was only seventeen years old), he related the dream to his eleven brothers (Gen. 37ff). They didn't find it so interesting.

"Behold," Joseph said, "we were out in the field gathering wheat and pressing it into sheaves and bundles. Suddenly, in my dream, I saw my sheaf stand up and I saw your sheaves bow down to mine!"

Now Joseph wasn't gloating; I doubt that he realized the full significance of the vision. But there was simply no way to relate that dream tactfully and without appearing to be extremely egotistical. The reaction of the brothers was natural. The Scriptures say that the brothers hated, even detested him. You can imagine your reaction if your brother claimed to have a dream in which you bowed down to him in an act of homage.

To compound the problem, Joseph had another dream. In this one, he saw "even the sun and moon and eleven stars bow down to me." It did not take much insight for the family to realize that the sun and moon represented the parents. The eleven stars were, of course, the eleven brothers. Even Jacob, a deeply spiritual man, questioned the validity of that one. But the Bible says he took it into his heart to consider it.

The brothers, on the other hand, took it to heart, but not to consider it. One day, as they watched Joseph coming toward them in the fields, they started talking.

"Who does he think he is?" one exclaimed. "He thinks he can get away with anything because our father loves him more than the rest of us."

"Behold, this dreamer cometh," they mocked.

"Let's teach him a lesson!" one brother whispered.

One of the brothers suggested killing Joseph. But the oldest brother, Reuben, who knew how dear the boy was to their father, intervened.

"Let's not shed blood," Reuben urged, "but let's just cast Joseph into that deep pit in the wilderness without food or water. That will be enough to teach him his lesson." Reuben, of course, planned to return secretly and rescue Joseph.

As you know from the story, the brothers agreed. As Joseph came near, they seized him, tore off his coat of many colors, and cast him into the pit.

While Reuben went off on an errand, the brothers sat down to eat bread and discuss the day's events. Suddenly, in the distance, they spotted a caravan of merchants winding slowly across the dusty plains of Canaan.

"I have an idea!" Judah exclaims. "What profit is there if we just let Joseph die in the pit? Let's sell him to the merchants! That way, we will get some money and at the same time be innocent of murder—after all, he is our own flesh and blood."

The brothers think that is a splendid idea. In Reuben's absence they haul the boy up out of the pit, and sell him to the merchants as a slave. When Reuben returned, the boy was gone. They dipped his coat in goat's blood and took it to Jacob, saying that a wild beast had devoured him. The brothers were pleased that Joseph was out of their way; Jacob in time reconciled himself to the boy's death; that was the end of Joseph.

Almost. When the merchants arrived in Egypt, they sold Joseph to an official named Potiphar, the chief of staff of Egypt's military forces. Although Joseph was now in a wealthy household, he was still a slave, the lowest person on the social scale. And by duplicity, he, a mere boy, had been forced from his home, where he was a direct descendant of the famous and revered Abraham.

We find some interesting Scriptures about Joseph's situation. "And the Lord was with Joseph, and he was a prosperous man; and he was in the house of his master the Egyptian. And his master saw that the Lord was with him and that the Lord made all that he did to prosper in his hand. . . . It came to pass from the time that he [Potiphar] had made him [Joseph] overseer in his house, and over all that he had, that the Lord blessed the Egyptian's house for Joseph's sake" (Gen. 39:2, 3, 5).

Does this mean that the Lord blessed Potiphar, a worshiper of pagan gods, just because of Joseph's presence in his house? Does this mean that God will honor and bless a business today because of the presence of just one Christian? Yes. Christ called us to be the salt and the light of the world—we bring flavor and light to the household of work. God will bless your unbelieving boss because of you.

So Potiphar noticed Joseph and saw that God was with him. Unfortunately, he wasn't the only one who noticed Joseph. Mrs. Potiphar did too and on numerous occasions tried to seduce him. Finally, one day, as it would happen, the house was empty except for the two of them. Mrs. Potiphar was in the kitchen, alone, and Joseph walked by. As he did, Mrs. Potiphar grabbed his coat and again propositioned him. Again he refused and rushed away, leaving Mrs. Potiphar with his coat.

Rejected and vengeful, Mrs. Potiphar, now in possession of Joseph's coat, devised a plan. When the servants came home, they found Mrs. Potiphar all upset. Joseph, the overseer of the house whom her husband had trusted, tried to rape her. She showed them his robe, which she tore trying to defend herself, she explained. Everyone was aghast. Potiphar came home and the story was repeated to him. In a rage, Potiphar threw Joseph into prison.

From a position of comfort and authority, Joseph was suddenly plunged into prison. And in those days, prison terms were highly indefinite. Men were tried and sentenced by the whim of the powerful and often simply left, sometimes forgotten, in prison to die.

But the Bible says that God was there, also, in prison with Joseph. "The Lord was with Joseph, and showed him mercy and gave him favour in the sight of his keeper of the prison" (Gen. 39:21). Even in that situation, God caused Joseph to prosper, and Joseph became one of the prison keepers himself.

At about the same time, two other men were thrown into prison. One was the Pharaoh's butler and the other, his baker. One morning, Joseph noticed that they looked extremely disturbed. It seemed that the two men dreamed strange dreams and could not fathom the meaning.

"Interpretation belongs to God," Joseph said encouragingly. "Tell me the dreams and perhaps God will reveal the meanings." They did; and God did. The butler, it turned out, would be set free and restored to his former position. The baker, however, would be hanged for what he did.

Three days later, these events came to pass, on the same day and in the same way as Joseph had said. As the butler, now free, was leaving the prison, Joseph cried out to him.

"Oh, lord," Joseph calls, "remember me to Pharaoh. Remember me, that I interpreted your dreams. I am in prison for no just cause!"

One would imagine that the butler would never forget Joseph; but he forgot him even as he walked out the door. Was he ungrateful? Perhaps, but that is not the main wrong that was done in this incident. Joseph called out in desperation for the butler's help. In desperation, we all look around and try to find a source of *human* help. Such-and-such a person, we reason, is in a position to help us; so we cry out to him for help. We call out to this person and that person, and as a result we are disappointed, hurt, and bitter against those we think have let us down.

But what does God say about depending on man for help? David prayed, "Give us help from trouble: for vain is the help of man" (Ps. 108:12). Isaiah wrote, "Woe to them that go down to Egypt for help . . . and trust in chariots, because they are many; and in horsemen, because they are very strong; but they look not unto the Holy One of Israel, neither seek the Lord (Isa. 31:1). And even stronger are these words of Jeremiah: "Cursed be the man that trusteth in man, and maketh flesh his arm . . ." (Jer. 17:5).

Joseph spent two more years in prison after calling out to the butler. Could Joseph's cry for help have cost him those two years? He wanted the butler to go running to Pharaoh to tell him of this wonderful, talented and *innocent* man he met in prison. Pharaoh, of course, would be duly impressed and would free Joseph. This is what Joseph was thinking. This is what Joseph wanted to happen. But where was God in the picture? Nowhere. God may or may not choose to deliver through people, but we are to look solely to Him, not to the people.

After the two years had passed, Pharaoh began having dreams. He called in all his wise men and all the soothsayers and the magicians, but no one was able to tell him the meaning of the dreams. One day a light bulb suddenly went on in the butler's head.

"I vaguely remember a man in prison," he told Pharaoh, "who told me the meaning of a dream I had . . . and it came true." Disgusted with all his high-paid court wise men, Pharaoh was willing to try a lowly prisoner with a good track record.

Joseph was called forth, cleaned and dressed in decent apparel to meet Pharaoh. Pharaoh related the dreams, for about the hundredth time, and as Joseph listened, God showed him the meaning.

"The seven fat cows are seven years of plenty," he informs Pharaoh, "and the seven lean cows are seven years of famine; the seven lean cows eat up the seven fat cows, like famine eats up plenty. . . ."

Pharaoh was amazed. He was so impressed that he sought Joseph's advice; he liked it so well, he exclaimed, "Is there any man in the kingdom as wise as Joseph?" And he proceeded to appoint Joseph ruler over all the land of Egypt.

By a sudden turn of events, Joseph was delivered from prison and made second-in-command of the kingdom, second only to Pharaoh himself. He is now far greater in power and wealth than his former boss, Potiphar. What do you think Mrs. Potiphar thought of that? Joseph had personal charge of the agriculture, which was the lifeline of the nation, and because he was in charge of storing and then distributing the food during the famine years, he actually held the power of life and death over the whole population.

For Better and for Worse

This is, I believe, a fair summary of Joseph's life—a dramatic one to say the least. We are familiar with the expressions, "we all have our ups and downs," or "behind every cloud is a silver lining." As Christians, we might say, "We all have our peaks and valleys." These are nice little homilies, but are they true?

Let's chart the topography of Joseph's life, and class each event or circumstance as better or worse than his life in Canaan. We will use Joseph's sheep-tending days as the starting point and measuring stick for determining how to class the other events.

THE CHRISTIAN EMPLOYEE

Joseph led a peaceful life with his family in Canaan. He had no severe problems, but he really had no responsibilities or future. He was the baby of the family and didn't have many opportunities. But his young life was rolling along smoothly for him—until the dreams came.

Suddenly, Joseph became a slave. Almost all of us would agree that this situation is a lot worse than being at home with the family, however unpleasant the family relationships might be. He had nothing and was carried away to a foreign country because of the treachery of his brothers.

Next, Joseph was promoted to the position of overseer in Potiphar's house. He had some degree of wealth and authority. He was the general manager of a small business. I believe this is a better situation than he had in Canaan, where he was only an errand boy and hated by his brothers.

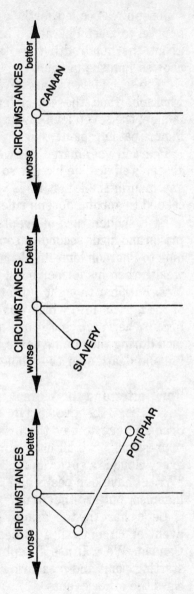

Next, Joseph was suddenly thrown into prison because of the false testimony of Mrs. Potiphar. He had nothing, no chance of appeal and little hope of ever getting out. Now, he was not only a slave in a foreign land, but a prisoner in a foreign land. The only reason we cannot chart this situation at absolute zero, rock bottom, is because he is at least alive and is made a prison trustee.

Lastly, Joseph was promoted to vice-president of Egypt. We can all agree that this was a wonderful turn of events. He was honored and respected by all the people, became a father to Pharaoh, and was avenged of all the injustices of his life. He held the reins of power in Egypt and had all authority and wealth at his disposal. The chart of his life is now complete.

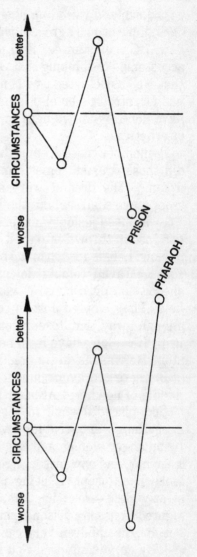

In the finished chart, the drastic changes in Joseph's circumstances are evident. He was cast down, raised up, cast down and raised up again.

God, we can all agree, elevated Joseph. But who cast him down? Circumstances? Evil people? Joseph's sins? We are accustomed to thinking that God places us on the peaks, but that He has deserted us when we enter valleys. Either God has forgotten us or else is punishing us for something we have done. What we need to know is that there is another alternative.

Remember those dreams the youthful Joseph had? Where did those dreams come from? God. God gave Joseph the dreams. The dreams were sound prophecy, which came true, as we shall see, but they served another purpose also. They aroused jealousy and hatred in the brothers. And that got Joseph thrown into a pit.

Now, here is Joseph in the pit. All of a sudden the brothers see a caravan coming down the road. But the brothers choose that pit because it was far away from any source of help. They wanted Joseph to die, so they chose a pit far enough away that Joseph couldn't be heard if he cried for help. It couldn't have been near a road, or a town, or a bus stop. He was out in the middle of nowhere.

But here a caravan bound for Egypt comes along out in the middle of nowhere. Accident?

God placed Joseph in the household of Potiphar, and everything went great for a while. Suddenly he was accused by an angry woman and cast into prison. First, a pit, then Potiphar, and now prison. From all outward appearances, it looks like Joseph is being punished for doing what was clearly right—resisting Mrs. Potiphar. All he gets for his righteousness is a prison term. Boy, God sure doesn't watch out for His children very carefully, does He?

Why do you suppose God slipped up and let Joseph get thrown in prison? Maybe so he could meet the baker and butler and interpret their dreams? Where did their dreams come from? God. After promptly forgetting Joseph, the butler suddenly remembered him two years later and referred him to Pharaoh. Where did Pharaoh's dreams come from? From God.

Suddenly the pieces of Joseph's life fall into place, revealing an intricate pattern. God gave him dreams, knowing he would tell all to his brothers, so He could arouse them to cast Joseph into the pit, so He could bring the caravan by at the right moment, so He could get Joseph to Egypt, so He could put him in Potiphar's household, so he could meet the baker and butler, so that the butler could refer him to Pharaoh, so Pharaoh could make Joseph ruler over all the land of Egypt!

If any one of these circumstances were omitted, then the whole chain of events would be broken. *Each circumstance was necessary to accomplish the end purpose*, which was to appoint Joseph over the land of Egypt. How does this concept affect our chart of Joseph's life? It shoots holes in it. If the pit, Mrs. Potiphar, and the prison were not mere chances of fate, bad luck or accidents, but in reality were engineered by God, then we must redraw the chart. The graph of Joseph's life cannot go up and down any longer. Why?

When Joseph's life is viewed from God's perspective, we see that all of the bad circumstances were actually God's vehicles to carry Joseph closer to apprehending God's plan for his life. When Joseph was in Canaan, God's vehicle of slavery drove up in the form of a caravan to carry Joseph to Potiphar. Mrs. Potiphar and prison were God's vehicles to carry Joseph before Pharaoh. Can you grasp the significance of this?

Paul knew this principle of spiritual progress when he wrote ". . . *all* things work together for good to them that love God, to them who are called according to his purpose."

THE CHRISTIAN EMPLOYEE

Do you love God? Are you dedicated to fulfilling His will for your life? If so, then *all* circumstances work together for your *good*, i.e., all circumstances are designed by God to elevate you spiritually to fulfill God's call on your life.

Our third principle, the principle of spiritual progress, is:

YOUR CIRCUMSTANCES ARE DESIGNED BY GOD

Using this principle, let's rechart Joseph's life.

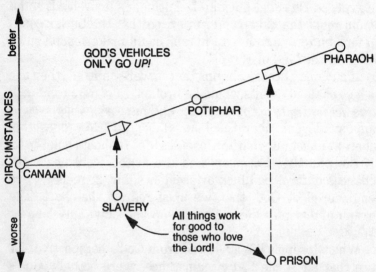

God is the architect of our circumstances. He designs each circumstance of life for our *good*, to take us higher and higher toward the goal He has for us. He looked upon Joseph and said, "I have ordained the plan and the man," and God set about to accomplish the goal.

But, you may ask, why does God use adverse circumstances? Why can't God's vehicles all be promotions, honors, raises, and none of them pits, Mrs. Potiphars, and prisons? Why couldn't God simply have spoken to Joseph and told him to go to Egypt? The answer to this question lies in the fact that God's dealings with men are multipurposed. God creates situations to do a work *in* us so that He can later do a work *through* us. The potter first fashions the clay into a vessel, according to the purpose of the potter, not those of the pot. Often the pits and prisons, the adverse circumstances, shape us and mold us into a useable vessel.

Another reason why God finds it necessary to design adverse circumstances is the proverbial problem with people—human nature. We humans are comfortable in ruts; in fact, we gravitate toward them. Ruts don't require much faith in God. Nothing disastrous can happen as long as we remain in the security of a rut.

Yet, Joseph was not wrong to stay in his rut in Canaan. His contentment in Canaan and in Potiphar's household were *good*. There is an expression, "Bloom where you are planted—then maybe God will move you to a bigger pot." This is exactly what happened to Joseph. He bloomed and prospered in every circumstance and God transplanted him to a bigger pot. It is *God's responsibility to move us*; we are to be content in every circumstance, confident of the fact that God designed our circumstances and will design another circumstance when He is ready to move us. And we are to be content when God uproots us and moves us to another place—that's where our affinity for ruts creates a problem.

We continually underestimate our potential in God. Moses felt incapable of leading the children of Israel out of Egypt; Gideon's fleece almost developed mildew before he finally obeyed God, and even then he felt more comfortable with his 32,000 soldiers than with God's 300. What if Joseph had refused to rule Egypt because he didn't feel capable? The small nation of Israel would have starved to death in short order.

THE CHRISTIAN EMPLOYEE

It is through adverse circumstances that God shows us that we are more than conquerors through Him. When it looks like our world is coming to an end because we are surrounded by adverse circumstances, that is when God says, "Watch me! Look what you can do through me." Your trust and faith in God deepens as you watch Him lead you through the trial.

It is as though God speaks to each person and says, "I have a special plan for your life. I have an important purpose and mission for you. It is not good that you should know what it is. Just serve me faithfully and trust me. You will go through hard times and trials, but each will be for your good. Will you believe?"

What if God appeared to you and said, "I have selected you to perform a mission for me. I am going to make you the moderator of the United Nations, and there, in that position, you will save the lives of millions of Americans and prevent two world wars?"

I imagine that you would start praising the Lord. You would answer, "O God, that's just great. Here I am. I am your servant. I will do anything you want me to."

Then, however, God says, "Fine. First, I am going to arrange for you to be thrown into prison on an unjust charge. I think I'll let Harry at the office accuse you of embezzlement. Then I'm going to arrange for you to get out after five years, but then your stock broker will make a mistake and you will go bankrupt and then. . . ."

Your enthusiasm would be a little dampened, no doubt, but you would still be willing, wouldn't you, *for the sake of the end goal*? This is actually how God speaks to us. God *has* told us that He has a special plan for each person. He *has* told us we will have trials and times of testing. And He has told us we would receive a crown.

The Crown

As we have seen, adverse circumstances are only God's vehicles to take us to Potiphar's household and the rulership of Egypt. We have examined Joseph's life and seen that his ups and downs were really only all ups.

There is another dimension to God's plan for each life, however. I'm sure the thought has occurred to many people that God cannot make every Christian the ruler of Egypt. God doesn't plan for every person to be the president of the United States. To this point, we have looked only at the specific adverse circumstances of Joseph's life but now we need to look at a deeper pattern.

> In James 1:12, we read: "Blessed is the man that *endureth temptation*; for when he is tried, he shall receive *the crown of life*, which the Lord hath promised *to them that love him*. (italics mine)

God's pattern of testing, followed by blessing, is an important truth which runs throughout the Bible. We Christians tend to view our lives as a series of peaks and valleys, yet God isn't leading us through a mountain range. *We do not have peaks and valleys, only testings and blessings.* It is imperative that Christians understand that God has a purpose for everything that happens to them.

The testing-blessing truth adds meaning to our lives and especially our adverse circumstances. God has promised a crown of life to the person who successfully endures adverse circumstances. Most people (including myself at one point) think that the crown of life refers to the crown we receive in heaven, but instead it means the crowns we collect here. Jesus said, "I have come that ye might have life and have it more abundantly." How do we obtain the abundant life? By standing trial, by enduring. Abundant life comes through the opportunities of adverse circumstances.

The secret to the overcoming and abundant life lies in your attitude toward adverse circumstances. When you face a trying situation, look just beyond it to the crown of life which God has promised to you if you endure that situation.

Joseph's life vividly illustrates the reality of the testing-blessing truth. Just beyond the vehicle of slavery was the crown of Potiphar's household. Just beyond the vehicle of prison was Pharaoh's crown. Our new and deeper chart of Joseph's life should look like this:

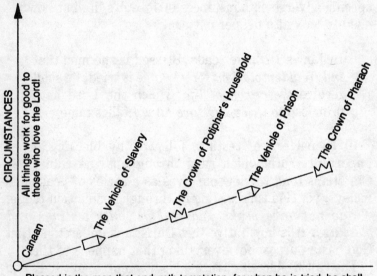

Blessed is the man that endureth temptation, for when he is tried, he shall receive the crown of life, which the Lord hath promised to them that love Him.

You see, God's vehicles don't just take us from one good circumstance to the next, like a bridge. They are times of testing and endurance that *result* in the crown of life, the next good circumstance.

This is why James could write, "My brethren, count it all joy when you fall into divers temptations." I used to read that

Scripture and think, "How can I possibly count trouble as joy?" But I would *try*. When I faced an adverse circumstance, I would grit my teeth and say, "Okay, Lord, it's joy." Needless to say, I wasn't very successful. I could not manufacture genuine joy—I was simply mouthing the words. But then God led me to the understanding that *"Blessed* is the man that endureth temptation: for *when he is tried*, he shall receive the *crown of life. . . ."*

God has told us of the crown that awaits the endurer. God wanted us to know about the crown—it is His incentive system. God doesn't want us to struggle in our adverse circumstances, wondering what is happening to us and why. He wants us to know that He has a crown for us when we have successfully endured. There is a vast difference between saying, "Somehow, I will make it. Somehow, God will bring me through this" (sometimes we add, "I *hope* . . ."), and saying, "Praise God, I'm standing trial. This is only a test to see how I react and endure. When the test is over, God will reward me with a crown!" *Only with this right attitude can we "count it all joy when we fall into divers temptation."* You can struggle all you like to be joyful, but until you can see that crown of life beyond the trial, you will not succeed.

While we Christians often speak of our limited frame of reference, we don't *really* understand how very limited our vision *really* is. While we see only our immediate situation, God sees our situation in the framework of His overall plan. While Joseph was tending sheep in Canaan, God saw *the Joseph who was ruling Egypt*. While Joseph was moving his family to Egypt, God had His eye on the Passover. While Joseph was busy enduring, God was looking all the way down the road of history to the great escape from Egypt, on to the Babylonian captivity, on to the crucifixion, and all the way to the second coming! Joseph played a leading role in this great drama of mankind because he endured the testings and received the crowns. I wonder how many Christians have lost a place in history because they refused to go through one small pit, one small testing! They could not see the crown beyond the trial.

Yet the Scriptures say, "Look to Jesus, the author and finisher of our faith, *who for the joy that was set before him endured the cross*, despising the shame, and is set down at the right hand of the throne of God. For consider Him that endured such contradiction of sinners against himself, lest ye be wearied and faint in your minds" (Heb. 12:2-3).

In the final chapters of Genesis, the outcome of Joseph's life is described. And if we read carefully, we see from the events that take place that God had *plural* purposes. He wanted to bless and exalt Joseph; He wanted to preserve the nation of Israel from the famine; but He had something else in mind also.

When the famine came to the land, only Egypt, of all the Old Testament nations, had food. Now all the nations flocked to Egypt to buy grain, and Joseph, who had been storing food for seven years, was ready to administer it to buyers.

Among the people who came to Egypt in hopes of buying grain was a family of Hebrews. They had heard that Egypt had food and had begged their father to let them go there. At first, the father resisted, for he had already lost one son and didn't want to risk losing another—after all, it was a dangerous journey into a dangerous land. But, in time, the threat of starvation at last became stronger than the threat of danger and the father finally gave his sons permission to go.

When they arrived in Egypt, they are directed to the great ruler of Egypt himself. They are admitted into his presence, bow humbly before him and present their request.

Joseph, known by his Egyptian name and dressed in his

rich Egyptian garb, is not recognized by the Hebrew family. But he recognizes them. He also recognizes in that moment that his childhood vision of the sheaves has been fulfilled, but that no longer seemed very important.

When Joseph is ready to reveal his identity, he is overcome with such emotion that he has to excuse himself to weep. That's odd. He's not overcome with fury, but with joy. He has not seen his family since he was seventeen years old and now he is a middle-aged man. After sending the guards from the room, he finally tells his brothers who he is.

"I am Joseph," he announces. "Doth my father yet live?" Well, the brothers just stare at him. He speaks again, "I am Joseph your brother, *whom ye sold into Egypt.*" The brothers still just stare. They already know how powerful this man—whom they had betrayed—has become.

I believe that Joseph had finally begun to grasp the plan of God for his life and to understand how God's purposes were accomplished through him. He had caught all the vehicles that took him higher in God. He revealed the fullness of his understanding in his amazing statement to his brothers, who stand quaking in fear before him:

"Now, therefore, be not grieved nor angry with yourselves, that ye sold me hither: for God did send me before you to preserve life [from the famine] . . . . And God sent me before you to preserve you a posterity in the earth, and to save your lives by a great deliverance. So now, *it was not you that sent me hither, but God*: and he hath made me a father to Pharaoh and lord of all his house, and a ruler throughout all the land of Egypt" (Gen. 45:5, 7, 8).

Joseph has realized that it was God who engineered his circumstances, led him through trials and led him to crowns. This wisdom was the something else God had in mind. God wanted Joseph to see the pattern in his life, to recognize the "great things God hath done."

THE CHRISTIAN EMPLOYEE

Joseph, as you know, tells the brothers to go home, bring back their father, and all their households, and come dwell with him in Egypt. Pharaoh, overjoyed at the reunion because of his love for Joseph, gives the family one of the best portions of land in the nation.

When Jacob finally discovered what his sons had done to his Joseph, he ordered them to go to Joseph and beg forgiveness—which they had not yet done. The brothers come before Joseph and fall on their faces at his feet. Again, Joseph reveals the depth of his understanding that God had arranged his whole life:

"Fear not: for am I in the place of God? But as for you, *ye thought evil against me; but God meant it unto good*, to bring to pass, as it is this day, to save much people alive."

This is a key statement. There is no more definitive statement in the Bible of the ideal attitude toward adverse circumstances than "ye thought evil against me; but God meant it unto me for good."

Consider the magnitude of Joseph's words. He had not forgotten his brothers' crime against him, for he repeatedly referred to himself as "your brother, whom ye sold into Egypt," and he spoke of their evil. Joseph didn't say, "Oh, that's okay. I understand. It wasn't so bad. Just forget it." No, he saw their action as a terrible wrong. Then why was he so kind? For two reasons: (1) ". . . am I in the place of God?" That is, it was not his responsibility to mete out judgment and punishment; and (2) he saw that God had accomplished a mighty work through him. Just because God uses the injustices and wrongs of men doesn't make the injustices and wrongs *right*, but it is *not* our place to punish and it *is* our place to recognize that "God meant it unto me for good."

Our circumstances in life will always be "up and down." We will always suffer from circumstances involving injustices, inequities, and unfairness. But an understanding that God has designed these circumstances for *our good* will set us free from our circumstances. So many people, including Christians, waste their lives, devoting all their energy and money, health, and strength, in trying to find that perfect niche, that Shangri-la. But no such thing exists. No set of perfect circumstances exist. God will not allow it. We all have thought before that we'd be happy if *only* this or that circumstance were different. Even if a person does manage to maneuver his circumstances to please himself, he won't be able to maintain his little universe for long—in time, his arrangement will crumble around his feet. The only solution is to have God's attitude toward adverse circumstances, to live on a level of life that transcends circumstances. This is the abundant life promised by Jesus.

The first step in adjusting your attitude to conform with God's attitude toward circumstances is to recognize His pattern in your life. Try making a chart of your own. Plot all the pits and Mrs. Potiphars and prisons. Plot all the rewards and crowns. Recognize where you are *now*. Most importantly, ask God to show you where you have a wrong attitude toward your adverse circumstances. You will never be free to live the abundant life until you recognize God designed your circumstances for your good.

The natural response to adverse circumstances, seemingly brought on by the injustices of men, is resentment. Resentment, if left untreated, will always evolve into bitterness. Are you bitter about that promotion you deserved but another received? About that sale that your co-worker took the credit for? About that failure that *you* got the credit for? About that time you were fired? The Scriptures say that many Christians are defiled by bitterness; bitterness colors and distorts a person's view of himself, others and God. As we have seen, depression is a symptom of the MMM Syndrome, and as it has been truthfully said, depression is the result of failing a test that God has brought into your life. The natural man sees his adverse circumstances as inflicted upon him by injustices of men; he is bitter toward them. And his own failure to successfully endure the trial results in depression.

The spiritual man, on the other hand, will not allow bitterness to take root in him. He, like Joseph, says, "you thought evil against me, but God meant it unto me for good." He realizes that God uses the pressure and heat of adverse circumstances to mold and purify His children so that they might become "vessels unto honor, sanctified and meet for the master's use, and prepared unto every good work." He understands that Jesus, "for the joy that was set before him endured the cross."

The spiritual man lives above the injustices and wrongs done to him by men, because he knows that God engineers all the circumstances of his life. The spiritual man understands God's testing-blessing pattern and collects his crowns of life.

Would you like your crown of life? God's vehicle will be by to pick you up in just a few minutes.

CHAPTER SEVEN

And Him Only Shalt Thou Serve

Another aggravating symptom of the MMM Syndrome is acute "classificationitis"—our human tendencies to *classify* our efforts and activities into one of two categories. We class our activities as either spiritual or secular, and "never the twain shall meet." Because we divide our activities, our activities *divide* us. We are torn between two worlds, and the result is turmoil.

When John's pastor called him aside after church one Sunday to ask if he would be willing to serve as a deacon, John felt an irrepressible surge of joy rise within him. Without hesitation, he said he'd *love* to serve as deacon and thanked his pastor heartily for the opportunity.

As he discussed the matter with his wife over Sunday dinner, John commented, "I've wanted to serve the church in some capacity for so long! God has answered my prayer. I'm so grateful for the opportunity." John proceeds to outline for his wife all the ways he plans to perform his duties.

The next morning—a Monday morning—just as John arrived at the office, his boss called him in for a conference.

"John," the boss begins, "you're one of the most dependable men I've got, and I want you to know that I appreciate your effort."

"Uh-oh . . ." John thinks. "What's coming now?"

"We've got to develop a special report for the board," the boss continues, "and present it at the meeting next month. That doesn't give us much time, but I know you can handle it. Of course, there may be some overtime involved, and you may have to work a couple of Saturdays but . . . ."

The more the boss talks, the lower John sinks in his chair. "Yes, sir," John mutters as he closes the door behind him.

"*We've* got to develop . . . *we* don't have much time . . ." he grumbles to himself. "It's going to end up being *me*, not *we*." By the time he reaches his desk, he isn't feeling the least bit spiritual. As he remembers the joy of Sunday, he sighs, "Yeah, the Apostle Paul was right—the things of the Spirit bring life but the things of the flesh bring death."

That night, John complains to his wife about the report he will have to do. "As if I don't already have a full schedule—more to do than anybody else in the office."

What has John done? Why did he jump at the opportunity to be a deacon, but balk at the *opportunity* to do a report? Obviously, it was because he classified his efforts into secular and and spiritual. Being a deacon directly involved service to the Lord; writing a report . . . well, that was service to the boss.

Or was it? Does God want us to divide our lives into secular and spiritual activities? Is this God's way of viewing our lives? *No.* In fact, *God makes no distinction between spiritual and secular work.* Our fourth principle of employment is, then:

YOU ARE EMPLOYED BY CHRIST, NOT BY YOUR COMPANY

Because John categorizes his activities into two realms, he himself is torn and divided. He sees himself trying to serve two bosses—Christ, who is his spiritual boss, and his secular boss. What is the result? He loves one and hates the other, and he sees no alternative to the problem.

Master

We often refer to Christ as our Lord and Master, but we tend to emphasize Lord while we breeze over the term Master. We just aren't accustomed to the master-slave relationship. Yet we do belong to Christ as slaves, purchased by His blood. We aren't owned by force against our wills, but neither are we free agents. We will either be slaves of sin or slaves of Christ.

Our problem is that we have confined the master role of Christ to the spiritual realm. We have limited His ownership of our lives to our spiritual activities. We need to adjust our attitudes to see that Christ, our employer, is master of our secular activities at work. This is expressed in this Scripture:

> Servants, obey in all things your masters according to the flesh; not with eyeservice, as menpleasers; but in singleness of heart, fearing God: and whatsoever ye do, do it heartily, as to the Lord, and not unto men; knowing that of the Lord ye shall receive the reward of the inheritance: for ye serve the Lord Christ. (Col. 3:22-24)

". . . *for ye serve the Lord Christ.*" The Word of God couldn't be much plainer. Whatever we do at work, we should do it heartily, as unto the Lord, because we are actually serving Him. Most of us would be embarrassed to present to God some of the work we have presented to our employers. John would probably be very reluctant to turn his report in to God, instead of his boss. Whatever we do at work, whether taking a client out to lunch, writing a report, or making a telephone call, we should do it enthusiastically, the same way we would gladly fulfill our spiritual responsibilities, whether serving as a deacon or Sunday school teacher. Are you able to sit at a typewriter or drafting board or in a meeting and know that you are serving the Lord? Can you realize that the letter you are writing for the boss or the advertising you are selling is just as spiritual as teaching Sunday school?

As we have seen, Jesus shed His blood on the cross for one particular purpose, and that was to purchase us, to pay a price for us. First Corinthians 7:23 reads: "Ye are bought with a price." Immediately following this statement, Paul adds: "Be not ye the servants of men." We are purchased slaves of Jesus, and therefore no one else can own us or demand service of us. We *owe* service to no man. We know that Jesus said, "Ye cannot serve two masters, for you will hate one and love the other, or love the other and hate the one." On the other hand, the Scriptures tell us to "obey in all things your masters according to the flesh. . . ." Do we have a dilemma? How can we serve our earthly masters and serve *only* Christ at the same time?

The answer lies in the fact that ultimately only Christ is our boss. We do not have an earthly master apart from Christ himself. This may seem to be just a game of semantics, or hair-splitting, but it is really of vast importance. How many people do you know who, when the boss walks in in the morning, see Jesus walking beside him? Not many, if any. Yet this truth must be a reality in our everyday lives if we are to be the employees Christ wants us to be.

Ed was having severe problems at work. The weekly grind had just about done him in. When he finally sat down with his pastor to discuss the situation, he announced that he had decided to go into full-time Christian work. Ed told the pastor that he felt God was definitely leading him out of secular employment and was calling him into a ministry.

When the pastor questioned Ed about the magnitude of his decision, Ed revealed that he had had three different jobs in the course of two years. All the jobs had been good ones, with respectable pay and positions, but Ed stated that he simply could not work with nonbelievers.

The pastor was surprised. He knew that Ed was a fine, devoted Christian, a good father and husband, and functioned well in all his church duties. After six years as a Sunday school teacher, the board had just appointed him as superintendent of the Sunday school department. The pastor knew that Ed was a capable, intelligent man, but he seemed to be hiding an undercurrent of anger when he spoke of his different jobs. The pastor wasn't convinced that God was calling Ed into the ministry.

With Ed's permission (and warning), the pastor called Ed's current supervisor after the counseling session ended, and received the following report: Ed was sullen, withdrawn, hard to work with, and refused to mix with his colleagues.

When the pastor asked Ed about this information at the next session, Ed exploded. "What did you expect him to say? That man isn't even a Christian and he doesn't believe in anything we stand for! I wish you could have heard the way he ridiculed me in front of the whole office staff the other day. Every time I try to say something to him about God, he says 'religion is only for women, children and the senile'—and of course he says it in a loud enough voice for everyone to hear. He uses the Lord's name in vain all the time and I have no respect for him at all . . . ."

The pastor questioned Ed about his other jobs. In each case, the problem was the same: the boss. Each boss had persecuted him for his beliefs when he tried to witness, and in turn, Ed had isolated himself. Because of the boss's disfavor, Ed would be assigned those jobs that irritated him; he would obey, but with grudging and smoldering anger. Finally, he had resigned from each job—usually to his boss's relief.

The pastor listened to Ed's tirade against his employers, then began sharing the scriptural injunctions about employment. He showed him Scripture after Scripture about serving the earthly master as unto the Lord.

Ed finally realized that his desire to go into the ministry was really a desire to escape from his problems at work. He went back to his current position and began to put the Scriptures into practice. It was difficult at first, because his boss expected him to try to cram the gospel down everyone's throat, then act like a martyr every time he was assigned a job. But after a short time, the boss began to notice that gradually Ed was becoming more cheerful and cooperative. The boss gradually stopped harassing Ed and began treating him with respect.

And every Sunday after church, Ed would pump the pastor's hand and exclaim, "It's working, pastor, it's working!"

One day the pastor got a call from Ed's boss. He wanted to make an appointment to discuss what movitation techniques the pastor had used on Ed. He had gone to management workshops and seminars for years to learn to motivate difficult employees, but he had never seen anything that worked like *this*. He was amazed at the changes in Ed, who had become the most conscientious and pleasant employee in the office.

When they met in the pastor's office, the pastor explained to Ed's boss the reality and validity of God's biblical truths, and how he had shared them with Ed. The boss was amazed. He had seen first-hand that God's truths *worked*.

The new understanding about the reality of God's ways did something to the boss. Eventually, Ed had his heart's desire—a Christian employer.

The Kingdom of Men

This brings us to the crucial matter of *authority* The Word says that all people, kings, princes, nobles and judges, who hold authority *hold it by the permission and sanction of Christ*. All authority, in other words, is of God and operates by God, and *there is no authority but God's authority*. "But," you may ask, "does this include my boss?" Most definitely. He has authority over you, doesn't he? Your superior has the authority over you to direct your activities, schedule, and salary. Any authority, held by anyone, to any degree, is God's authority. God has ordained all authority, regardless of whether or not those using that authority recognize Him as God. Remember Cyrus? God called Cyrus, who was a pagan conqueror, "*My* shepherd . . . whose right hand *I am holding*." God had directed Cyrus's life in specific ways, long before Daniel unrolled before him that scroll with his name in it, when Cyrus became a believer.

We are more or less aware of a spiritual hierarchy in the kingdom of God. Jesus, the King of kings, is at the right hand of the Father; below Him are His angels and saints. We know that the angels have an order, with Michael being an archangel, and other angels being chief princes. Among the saints, too, we recognize leaders, tried and proven men of God, including many of our nationally known Christian figures. Within each local church, Christians hold offices of

101

bishops, pastors, elders, deacons and teachers, each with varying degrees of authority. We know that every position held, official or not, is important to the body of Christ, but clearly some positions hold more authority than others. As Christians, we recognize, respect, and fit into this chain of command within the church. We recognize that God has set leaders in the church to be our spiritual superiors. It is respect for greater spiritual authority that keeps the church from being spoiled by immature and unwise people who would inadvertently lead the people into error. We accept and are grateful for God's chain of command in the church.

But what happens when we leave for the office? We ignore and belittle our secular superiors. We fight against their authority. We complain about their decisions. We criticize their work. God has a chain of command for the secular world, that is, like the spiritual chain of command, for our good. But we think that because work is secular, we can act like our own little kings, entitled to rule the kingdom as we see fit. We treat the boss in ways we would never dream of treating the pastor. God, we think, doesn't care about the office.

That God cares about authority at the office and in all secular realms is clear from several Scriptures. God's regard for secular authority—because it is His authority—is shown repeatedly throughout His Word. Look at this one, for starters:

> Let every soul be subject unto the higher powers [authorities].* For there is no power [authority] but of God: the powers [authorities] that be are ordained of God. Whosoever therefore resisteth the power [authority], resisteth the ordinance of God: and they that resist shall receive to themselves damnation. For rulers are not a terror

to good works, but to the evil. Wilt thou then not be
afraid of the power [authority]? do that which is
good, and thou shalt have praise of the same: For
he is the minister of God to thee for good. (Rom.
13:1-4)

So often, the very things we Christians fight against are
for our own good, and secular authority is one of them. Stop
and think for a moment about all the authorities you
encounter in life. If you listed all the people who exercise
authority over you, you would be amazed. You would have
to include everyone from the president of the United States
down to the local policemen. You would have to list senators,
congressmen, bureaucrats in the IRS, each member of the
local city council, the mayor, the judges, the city dogcatcher,
and innumerable others. Ponder the fact for a moment that
you are to be subject to each one of these people.

Why are authority and submission to authority good for
us? Why is the local policeman a minister of God to us for
good? It seems contrary to all thinking, because the
authorities, including the boss and the local man in blue,
seem determined to rob us of the freedom to do things our
way.

To discover the answer, we must examine the human
attitude toward authority. Let's take, for example, your
attitude toward the local policeman, whom we'll call Hank.

When you are driving along and catch a glimpse of Hank in
your rear-view mirror, how do you react? You immediately
look down at your speedometer, don't you? Even if you're
not speeding, you check the speedometer, *just in case.* And
even if you're not speeding, you don't really relax until Hank

has turned off in another direction and you are safely out of his range of vision. You react this way, even though you were not doing anything wrong.

Why? It is because we are aware of the *presence of authority*. Hank is not only another man equal with you in the eyes of God, but he is also an officer of the law.

Would you change your driving habits if Hank were assigned to follow you around all the time? In all probability, you would. Good and lawful driving habits would become second nature to you and that policeman would no longer pose a threat—*because you would be accustomed to the presence of authority*.

The variable in your driving habits would not be the law, but the presence of one who can enforce the law. No matter how often you drive seventy miles an hour, the speed limit is still fifty-five miles an hour. No matter how often you slip through a red light, the law still demands that you stop. In other words, Hank did not suddenly create the law when he appeared behind you with his blue light flashing. The law was always the same. It was the presence of a man who could enforce that law that makes the difference in your driving. Even if you never get caught when you speed, you are still going against the authority of law.

When we realize that all authority is ordained by God—blessed, sanctioned and approved—and is not just a decree from human beings in Washington, D.C., our attitude toward authority should change drastically. It was God who passed the fifty-five-mile-an-hour speed limit law. It was God who decreed that we should stop at red lights. Are those laws good? Clearly, yes. Who hasn't seen the results of breaking the law—smoldering remains on the side of the road, obituaries, and broken bodies?

A rebellious attitude toward authority is, essentially, a statement that "I am not in need of controls. I am perfectly capable of driving this automobile as I see fit." We are all guilty of this attitude, not only in driving, but in virtually every phase of our lives. We have an innate desire to control what we do as we see fit. Rebellion has, especially today, crept into our thinking against every figure of authority and institution we have. Indeed, rebellion has been dressed up and disguised and sanctioned in the name of interested citizenship, getting involved, political activism, and even humanism. The most extreme (and deceptive) disguise is "doing your own thing." But no matter how we dress rebellion up in fancy attire, it's still the proverbial sow's ear. Adhering to your beliefs is one thing; rebellion is quite another. Just as we can see rebellion in our children, God can see it in His.

If you tell your son Johnny that he cannot ride his bicycle in the busy streets, he will most likely tell you that he will be careful, that he knows all the rules of safety, and that he, after all, is not a child anymore. But if you are a wise parent, these arguments will not sway you. You will still insist that he cannot ride in the street. And he knows what will happen if he disobeys—if he doesn't get hurt in the street, he will when he gets home!

God is just as adamant about His rules as human parents are about their rules and for the same reason. Parents enforce rules because they desire to protect their children from themselves. Rules, set by authorities, are for our good. Some rules may protect us from dangers that we cannot readily see. A child, for instance, cannot see the slightest sense in bedtime rules. A child can stay up until ten at night and then jump out of bed at the crack of dawn with nary a yawn—but what about the next night, or the next night? Their work at school will not be up to par; they develop deep circles under their eyes; they fall asleep right in the middle of arithmetic, and so on. Likewise, God sets authority over us for reasons—good reasons—that we cannot discern with our limited wisdom. No matter how insignificant a rule may seem—some small regulation at the office, for example—the authorities who set and enforce that rule are servants of God for your good.

What happens to people who resist authority? According to the Word of God in the Scriptures we have examined, those who resist authority incur judgments. We know that people who resist the authority of God all their lives, in refusing the gospel, will receive judgment eternally. But there are a hundred and one ways to receive it here and now. Prisons are full of people who resisted authority by breaking laws. They rebelled against authority and received unto themselves twenty years in the slammer. Others, even Christians, end up in traffic court, or worse. At the office, we can be harassed, like Ed was, or even fired, for rebelling against the authority of the boss.

Most of us don't complain about policemen unless we have just received a ticket. We complain somewhat more about elected officials, but most of all, we complain about the boss. Sit in on any office party and, sooner or later, the conversation will get around to the subject of the boss. More than any other authority figure, his actions dominate and control our time at the office—which, as we have mentioned, consumes most of our waking hours. The boss exerts tremendous influence and authority over us. But if we are to learn fully of the kingdom of God on earth, we must understand fully that all the power and authority the boss holds is from God and God alone. The boss, we must learn, is the minister of God for our good.

When we say the Lord's prayer, we repeat the phrase, "Thy kingdom come, thy will be done, on earth . . . ." We pray that God will rule His kingdom *here* as He does in heaven. But how can we pray for God's kingdom to come to earth, while we reject His authority on earth? We want His will, but not His orders. We want Him to rule our lives, but won't accept the chain of command which God is using to rule our lives.

When the centurion asked Jesus to only speak the word and his servant would be healed, he added an important statement: "For I am a man under authority. I tell one to go and he goes; I tell another to come, and he comes." He recognized Jesus' authority, and as a man under authority he also possessed authority.

Look at what Jesus answered: "So great a faith I have not seen in all of Israel."

God has surrounded each of us with authorities for a purpose. He could have ordained anarchy and made it function, but He didn't. God uses authority *to work into our natures a submissiveness and obedience.* We come into this world screaming and kicking and demanding the fulfillment of our every whim, and we are really outraged when we soon find our little egos being challenged by mother. "How dare that woman defy my wishes!" we think, in our little protected world of soft diapers, milk on demand, and sanitation service every time we feel like it. But soon, the conspiracy has spread from mother and daddy to teacher—and then principals and policemen and on and on it goes. If you think you can go through life with that same basic attitude toward authority—and then graduate to heaven—you are badly mistaken. What was Satan's sin? *Rebellion.* And as we have seen from the episode of Korah, rebellion has a way of spreading like wildfire. Satan's rebellion spread to infect a third of the angels in heaven. We cannot go through life screaming and kicking against authority and expect God to open wide the pearly gates to let us in—to infect others. Heaven is a place of total submission, and we won't like it if we aren't already submissive.

THE CHRISTIAN EMPLOYEE

God wants us to become so accustomed to submitting to authority that we relax, obey (without having to debate with ourselves), and enjoy the results. "Whoso keepeth the fig tree shall eat the fruit thereof: so he that waiteth on his master shall be honoured" (Prov. 27:18).

"Exhort servants to be obedient unto their own masters, and to please them well in all things; not answering again [talking back], not purloining, but showing all good fidelity; that they may adorn the doctrine of God, our Saviour, in all things" (Titus 2:9-10). That doesn't sound much like today's philosophy of democracy and equality, does it? No, but heaven isn't democratic, either. It is theocratic.

Another Scripture that reveals to us the mind of Christ on the matter of the boss and his authority is found in 1 Peter 2:18-21:

> Servants, be subject to your masters with all fear; not only to the good and gentle, but also to the froward. For this is thankworthy, if a man for conscience toward God endure grief, suffering wrongfully. For what glory is it, if when ye be buffeted for your faults, ye shall take it patiently? but if, when ye do well, and suffer for it, ye take it patiently, this is acceptable with God. For even hereunto were ye called: because Christ also suffered for us, leaving us an example, that ye should follow his steps.

Clearly God makes no distinction between the good master and the bad master, and neither can we. God backs the boss whether he is godly or ungodly, fair or unfair. Paul wrote that Jesus was obedient unto death. But after the suffering and the death, comes the resurrection. God always rewards obedience to authority, because it is actually obedience to Him.

The trial of Jesus, according to lawyers who studied it, could not have been more illegal or unfair. Christ was denied His rights, tried by the wrong people, at the wrong place, at the wrong time. Everything about the trial was illegal. His enemies railroaded a verdict before anyone could come to Jesus' defense.

After agonizing in the Garden of Gethsemane, Jesus was captured, beaten, scourged, and had a crown of thorns pressed deeply into his forehead. (This treatment, too, of any prisoner was illegal.) As Jesus stood before Pilate, He was emotionally and physically exhausted, yet His obedience to the Father stood steady. Pilate had asked Jesus question after question, but received no answer. Finally, in exasperation, Pilate exclaimed, "Why don't you answer me? Don't you know I have the authority to crucify you and the authority* to release you?"

Look at Jesus' amazing answer to Pilate: "Thou couldest have no power[authority] at all against me, except it were given you from above" (John 19:11). As Jesus faced the Roman government, it was the Father to whom He was submitting. And in the face of outrageous injustices, Jesus still submitted.

At the trial and the crucifixion, Jesus suffered alone. All of His friends, supporters, the crowds which had followed Him, even His own disciples had deserted Him. At times in our lives, the ultimate in loneliness will happen to us also. We will feel a loss of strength and even confidence in God which we derive from our Christian compatriots.

But Jesus said, "If any man serve me, let him follow me; that where I am, there shall my servant be also." Think about this for a moment. Where I am, there shall my servant be also. Jesus doesn't follow us around; we follow Him. So if we're at the office, Jesus must have been there first. We

THE CHRISTIAN EMPLOYEE

don't walk into the office, just hoping maybe we can emerge from the day with a little of our spirituality intact. We follow Jesus into the office, and if we will let Him, He will lead us every step through the day.

When you look at your boss next week, picture Jesus standing directly behind him. If you can do this for one week, your attitude toward your boss should change drastically. The artificial gap between your spiritual work and your secular work will begin to close. We know that Jesus is "the same yesterday, today and forever," and we love to remember that the same Savior who walked on the earth two thousand years ago is the same one we follow today. But somehow we can't quite grasp the significance of His sameness. We assume that by "yesterday" in this Scripture, Paul somehow meant two thousand years ago. But just maybe Paul meant literally that Christ is the same *yesterday*, today and forever. Jesus is the same on Monday as He was on Sunday. He is the same on Friday as He was on Thursday.

If you will cease confining God to the weekend, or to the day when you feel especially spiritual, and expect Him to meet you at work on Monday morning, you will no longer divide your world—or yourself. If you look to God to be Lord of the weekday as He is Lord of the sabbath, the result will be wholeness in your life and attitude toward work. As you invite God to be God of the whole week, you will be a whole man, recognizing that God's authority over your life comes through the pastor—and the boss.

". . . God . . . is the blessed controller of all things, the king over all kings, and the master of all masters. . ." (1 Tim. 6:15 Phillips).

---

* The word "authority" has been substituted for the King James Version "power" since it is a more accurate translation of the original Greek text.

CHAPTER EIGHT

The Danger of the Deadly Member

Another symptom of MMM Syndrome is a critical attitude toward the boss. Rather than a visual malfunction, this is a mental deficiency. The criticisms which begin in the mind usually end up in the mouth, since we cannot prevent our attitudes from becoming actions.

Jack and Caroline were visiting Wayne and his wife, Joyce, on a Saturday afternoon. Joyce invited them to stay for a cookout later in the evening. After the meal, while the girls were clearing away the dishes, Jack and Wayne began talking.

Jack had been a Christian for just over a year. He had a great deal of respect and admiration for Wayne, who was an elder in his church. He had, in fact, been waiting for an opportunity to discuss a problem that had really bothered him lately. When Wayne asked, "Did you have a good week?" Jack unloaded.

"Well," he said, "I don't know. I've felt sort of—dry lately. I can't explain it, really. I know the Lord's still there, but my prayers just don't seem to get through lately. Even church is beginning to be, well, boring."

Wayne, whom Jack had confided in on several occasions, began to probe. He asked Jack about his marriage, the kids, church, then work. When he mentioned work, Jack's response told him that he had found the problem area. Jack described to him a scene that occurred almost daily at coffee break.

All the men in Jack's office gather around one table for coffee to catch up on news. A couple of the secretaries join them and everyone begins to talk about the wives, husbands, kids, etc. But it isn't long before the conversation comes around to the boss.

"You know, at that last staff meeting," Frank says, "Jim really blew it. He had a golden opportunity to set the record straight about the real cause of that bottleneck in production—the maintenance department can't keep an adequate supply of machine parts to keep the plant running. . . ."

"I know it," Bill adds, "every time a piece of equipment breaks down, we have to stand there and wait until the part is shipped in—from Atlanta. That always takes about a week. No wonder we're always behind. . . ."

"Not only that," Janet adds, "but you know, don't you, that he blames it on *you*. He sent a memo to Mr. McMurphy last week trying to explain the delay and he said, his exact words were, 'Due to a failure of our production supervisor to. . . .' "

Bill's face turned as red as a beet.

"Well, you know that is just like him. . . ." This time, it is Jack's turn. He has been sitting quietly, but he could hold back no longer; the more he listened, the more agitated he became.

"He never stands up for any of his employees," Jack explodes. "He could have gotten the company to buy those safety shoes for our boys, but when the vice-president told him things were a little tight with the budget, Jim gave right in. He even said that his people would be glad to buy their own shoes!"

"Yeah," Tom says sarcastically, "we'd just be thrilled to fork out twenty-five dollars. . . ."

Another secretary feels that she has some light to throw on the situation.

"You know why he did that," she says with a knowing look. "There's an opening coming up in marketing when Mr. Johnson retires and Jim is buttering up the brass to get the position. . . ."

And so on and on the conversation went. Jim was placed under the employees' microscope and his every word and action scrutinized. Invariably the conclusion was the same—Jim doesn't measure up to his employees' standards.

"It's such a little thing," Jack concluded. "I don't know why it bothers me, but after a coffee break session like this, I just feel uneasy. Everything we say about him is true, but still, after I say those things about him, I just feel a little, well, dead inside. . . . Oh, well, I know it isn't important. . . ."

As Jack talked, Wayne remembered a particular Scripture which he felt was applicable to Jack's situation and he shared it with him.

God and His Doctrine

As we have seen, your employer exercises authority over you and his authority is from God and God alone. As we have also seen, God engineers every minute detail of our lives. This means that *God* has placed your employer—your particular employer, with all his faults and personality flaws—over you.

Paul writes, by the inspiration of the Holy Spirit, "Let as many servants as are under the yoke count their own masters worthy of all honor. . . ." Why? Paul tells us in the next phrase, ". . . *that the name of God and his doctrine be not blasphemed*" (1 Tim. 6:1).

Our fifth principle is, then:

COUNT YOUR SUPERIORS WORTHY OF HONOR IN THOUGHT, WORD AND DEED

This principle probably cuts to the quick in most Christians. We have all been guilty of criticizing the boss. We sit back and analyze his decisions, make jokes about his peculiarities behind his back, and love to talk about what we would do if we were in his place. But we *aren't* in his place.

Far from counting our superiors worthy of honor, we have decided that he, of all people, is not worthy of honor. Yet, according to the Scriptures, *we are guilty of blasphemy when we do not honor the boss.* Most of us would not dare blaspheme God. We have reverent fear of God and His power, even when we fully understand His long-suffering, love, and willingness to forgive. We are afraid to speak against God and would not dare criticize Him, yet we have no qualms whatsoever about criticizing and speaking maliciously against the boss. We bellyache over every decision handed down to us by the boss. We think he's the most incompetent individual in the history of the company. We frequently say, "How in the world did he ever get to that high position? He is simply incapable of handling such responsiblility!" All these ways in which we dishonor the boss are exactly the same as shaking our fists at God and calling Him incompetent. You are telling God that he can't do His job right.

Again, some people will object. "How can God mean for us to honor a boss, regardless?" Does God mean that we should honor an unbelieving boss? The very next verse after Paul's instructions to honor the boss, he writes, "And them that have believing masters, let them not despise them, because they are brethren; but rather do them service . . ." (1 Tim. 6:2). That means Paul was referring to unbelieving masters in the previous verse.

Look at Paul when he was brought before the Sanhedrin for preaching the gospel. The Sanhedrin was a court composed of Jewish lawyers and theologians—the Pharisees and Sadducees. The charge against Paul on this occasion was heresy (Acts 23). As Paul began his defense, by telling the Sanhedrin that he had always had a clear conscience before God, one of the lawyers took offense at his remarks and ordered a guard to strike Paul. So, while Paul was speaking away, the guard hauled off and hit Paul across the mouth.

Feisty little Paul wheeled around to the lawyer who gave the order and said, "Why you whitewashed hypocrite! May God strike you!" He was about to really let that man have it, when another lawyer interrupted. The lawyer exclaimed, "Do you dare revile the high priest?"

Look closely at Paul's reaction. He answered, "Brothers, I did not know that he was the high priest. For it is written, 'Thou shalt not speak evil of the ruler of thy people.'" When he found out that the lawyer was the high priest, he apologized because of the high position of the lawyer.

Obviously, the high priest was not worthy of honor. No one had more right to criticize those religious leaders than Paul. He had once been one of them, and knew that they were not so much concerned with finding out if Jesus was the long-awaited Messiah as they were with maintaining their legalistic doctrinal system. If anyone should have known that Jesus was the Messiah, it was those religious leaders. From the human point of view, Paul was right to expose the hypocrisy of the high priest; but he knew that from God's point of view, that high priest was an authority set over the people for their good. Paul bowed to God's authority represented in the high priest. He honored a man who was unworthy of honor and indeed a man at whose hand he had just suffered an injustice by being struck unlawfully. Even though this high priest was actually an enemy of the gospel, his authority still came from God and Paul knew it.

Another startling case of the recognition of God's authority involved King Saul and the young man, David. Suffering from a case of guilty conscience and paranoia, Saul had come to fear and hate David, whom the people loved. He believed that the young shepherd was trying to usurp his throne.

Saul, as you will recall, had disobeyed God and fallen away from following Him. When God sent a prophet to confront Saul, the king simply insisted that he had done nothing wrong. He would not repent. As a result, God withdrew from Saul, and told the prophet Samuel that He was sorry He had ever made Saul king of Israel. At that time, God also revealed to Samuel that He had already chosen David as the next king. After a while, David also realized that God had chosen him as the next king; the people understood this, and Samuel knew it, of course; and Saul was beginning to get the idea.

Saul began to hunt David down like game. But instead of confronting the king, David ran—and ran and ran. He fled into the mountainous wilderness and collected a band of rabble about himself.

On one occasion, as David was fleeing for his life, he found a cave in which to hide. Hot on his heels, however, Saul stopped in the general vicinity of the cave to search the area. He spotted the cave and went into it to relieve himself.

Hiding in the rear of the cave, David and his men knew this as a perfect opportunity to rid themselves of the enemy.

"Behold the day of which the Lord said unto thee, Behold,

I will deliver thine enemy into thine hand," one soldier whispers to David, "that thou mayest do to him as it shall seem good unto thee. . . ."

Instead of killing him, David slipped up, and stealthily cut off a piece of Saul's skirt and slipped away again. But then, "it came to pass afterward, that David's heart smote him, because he had cut off Saul's skirt. And he said unto his men, The Lord forbid that I should do this thing unto my master, the Lord's anointed, to stretch forth mine hand against him, seeing he is the anointed of the Lord" (1 Sam. 24:5-6).

In the meantime, Saul had left. When David realized his wrong, he went out of the cave and called to the king. When Saul looked back, David asked the king why he believed the counselors who told him that David was seeking his life. Then he showed him the piece of skirt he cut off, and told him what had happened in the cave to prove that the king had nothing to fear. David called upon God to avenge him but promised Saul he would not harm him. Then Saul "lifted up his voice and wept."

This was an amazing incident. Even Saul said, "If a man find his enemy, will he let him go well away?" But the enemy in this case was "the Lord's anointed," the man God had chosen to rule Israel.

On another occasion (Saul didn't stay appeased very long), David again was being hunted down. This time, David sneaked into camp one night, and took the king's spear, which was stuck in the ground beside his head. Again, David has advisers.

"God hath delivered thine enemy into thine hand this day," whispered Abishai, a soldier-follower of the future king. "Now therefore let me smite him, I pray thee, with the spear even to the earth at once, and I will not smite him the second time" (1 Sam. 26:8).

"Destroy him not," David answered, "for who can stretch forth his hand against the Lord's anointed and be guiltless?

As the Lord liveth, the Lord shall smite him; or his day shall come to die; or he shall descend into battle and perish. The Lord forbid that I should stretch forth mine hand against the Lord's anointed . . ." (1 Sam. 26:9-11).

The next morning, David called out to Abner, the chief adviser to the king, and berated him for his neglect. "As the Lord liveth," he shouted, "ye are worthy to die, because ye have not kept [protected] your master, the Lord's anointed!"

This went on for years. At times, David had to flee the country. One would think he would get tired of the whole business. I'm sure he did, but he would not touch the king, no matter what the king did to him. It wasn't that David was so confident that he would become king or that the Lord would not allow Saul to kill him. He was simply determined to honor God's authority, even unto death.

You see, God had withdrawn His Spirit from Saul's heart and life, but He had not yet withdrawn His authority from Saul. Saul was still the king of Israel. Saul's spiritual condition was none of David's concern. David didn't honor Saul for his condition, but for his position. David did not see Saul as a fallen, pathetic figure of a man, but as the mighty king of Israel, appointed by God, and to whom therefore honor and respect were due.

David was determined that he would let God pull down one and set up another. He did not help God out by killing Saul. He recognized that Saul was the minister of God to him for good. Now wait a minute! Saul was the minister of God to David for good? Yes. It was for David's good that he spent years submitting to an authority who was actually trying to take his life. Those years were training, preparation, and testing for David, and he passed with flying colors.

Because of David's faithfulness and submission, look at how God exalted him. Many of the prophecies concerning the coming Messiah referred to David's obedience and love for God. The Messiah was the seed of David, the son of David, the star of David, coming to reign on the throne of David. The Scriptures even call David a man after God's own heart (Acts 13:22). Not before or since has the nation of Israel had a greater king.

The Carnal Mind

After Wayne had explained the principle of counting your superiors worthy of all honor, he illustrated it with the lives of Paul and David. Jack had listened intently, recognizing the truth of Wayne's words.

"Jack," Wayne continued, "it is not only important that you understand God's principles concerning your boss, but it is equally important that you understand what happened to you spiritually because of those discussions about the boss."

Jack looked confused.

"Earlier, when we began talking, you said that you had been spiritually dry and that after the conversations at coffee break you felt dead inside."

Jack nodded in agreement.

"The dryness and death," Wayne continued, "were a result of your returning to old patterns of thought that you had before you met Christ. Romans 8:6 says 'To be carnally minded is death; but to be spiritually minded is life and peace.' When you joined in with others in criticizing your boss, you became carnally minded—and it produced its fruit in you—death."

Jack realized that this was exactly what had happened to him. "I understand what you're saying," he said.

"The Scriptures have given us an antidote for carnal mindedness," Wayne explained. "Paul wrote, 'Be renewed in the spirit of your mind'; and 'We have the mind of Christ'; and also, 'Let this mind be in you which was also in Christ

THE CHRISTIAN EMPLOYEE

Jesus.' When we come to the Lord, we must have our minds reprogrammed. God said, 'My thoughts are not your thoughts; neither are my ways your ways.' As we allow God, He will teach us to think His thoughts. And the Scriptures make it plain to us how He thinks about our superiors. God wants us to honor and obey them because He has placed them in their positions—does this make sense to you?"

Jack leaned back in his chair and sighed. "Yes," he answered, "but it's pretty heavy stuff. The whole idea is so new to me—and so contrary to our thinking today. . . ."

"I just thought of another Scripture," Wayne said, " 'Let no corrupt communication proceed out of your mouth, but that which is good to the use of edifying, that it may minister grace unto the hearers' " (Eph. 4:29).

Jack had to admit that those coffee break "communications" didn't minister grace to anyone.

"And I just thought of another one," Wayne exclaimed, laughing, ". . . it's just that there are so many Scriptures on this subject . . . but I can't remember exactly how this one goes. . . ."

After Wayne retrieved a Bible from his house, he opened it to Ecclesiastes 10:20 and handed it to Jack. Jack read, "Curse not the king, no not in thy thought; and curse not the rich in thy bedchamber: for a bird of the air shall carry the voice, and that which hath wings shall tell the matter."

"That's true," Jack said. "Things do have a way of getting back to people, don't they?"

The Deadly Member

It is no wonder that James wrote: "The tongue can no man tame; it is an unruly evil, full of deadly poison. Therewith bless we God, even the Father; and therewith curse we men, which are made after the similitude of God" (3:8-9). We have "forked tongues," in other words.

The Danger of the Deadly Member

If we are honest with ourselves, we will admit that the tongue is one of the hardest things to control in our Christian walk. If some of us Christians couldn't talk about other people, we wouldn't have anything to say. We have made other people our verbal diet for so long that we find ourselves literally speechless at times if we excluded people's faults from our conversations. It is so easy to find ourselves in a discussion about others, their shortcomings, etc. "But," we reason, "what we say about people is true. We don't gossip and spread lies; we are simply relating the truth . . . why can't we discuss it?" The Scriptures repeatedly tell us, however, that the follower of Christ must not participate in character evaluations or assassinations of others. Try, for just one day, not to speak about a third person in the presence of a second person. It's an eye-opening experience.

As Jack began putting the principle of honoring your boss into operation at work, he soon discovered another truth. Not only was his conscience sensitive to every slip of his tongue, but he found that even when he did not join in the usual coffee break discussions, the spiritual dryness, although considerably diminished, still continued. After praying about the situation, he saw that simply listening to derogatory discussions was no different than actively joining in. He saw that he actually wanted to listen to the failures and shortcomings of his boss and others. God showed him that he used these discussions in a vain effort to elevate his opinion of himself.

At the next coffee break, when the usual roast-the-boss began, Jack excused himself and returned to his desk. As he left the group, he sensed the presence of the Holy Spirit in a dimension he had never before experienced. Jack knew that he had found the heart of God, the mind of Christ, and as a result, joy welled up inside.

THE CHRISTIAN EMPLOYEE

On-The-Job Conflicts

"Okay, I agree," some readers are probably thinking, "that the Lord wants me to learn to control my tongue and honor my boss with my words—or lack of them—but how should I handle those conflicts with my boss that occur from time to time?" Are we simply to sit back and do nothing when injustices and misunderstandings occur? Are we never to communicate our dissatisfaction over a situation or discuss a problem with our superiors? If not, how do we handle the situation without dishonoring the boss? The Word tells us exactly what to do.

Let's assume that a problem has arisen between you and your boss. It may involve your work load, something the boss has said or done, or some misunderstanding or miscommunication that has occurred. Whatever the problem, you feel that the boss is in the wrong, and the consequences could be significant.

The scriptural principle of resolving conflicts within the church body can be applied here as well. "If thy brother shall trespass against thee, go and tell him his fault between thee and him alone: if he shall hear thee, thou hast gained thy brother" (Matt. 18:15). After prayerfully reviewing the situation and examining yourself to see if there are any personal failures which may have contributed to the problem, you should then approach your boss for a private talk. But if you are guilty of any offense, however slight, the Lord requires that you first make it right by confessing it to him and asking him for forgiveness (Matt. 5:23-24).

After your conscience is clear of personal offense, discuss the problem with your boss alone. You cannot air the offense to the whole office and then expect God to bless your conversation with the boss. Be frank but not condemning in your approach as you explain the problem to him. You might begin the discussion something like this: "Jim, I know that you were angry with me yesterday. I want to correct any shortcoming that I have and I would appreciate it if you would point out where I've failed you or my work." This approach opens communication and also allows him to point out blind spots you have in viewing your own actions and attitudes. Listen to him with an open mind and take whatever steps are necessary to correct any deficiencies he might point out.

In the process, your superior will explain, in all likelihood, why he was angry with you and will appreciate you for your concern. By handling conflicts in this biblical fashion, you will be amazed at the results. If you've done nothing to provoke an attack, in all probability he will apologize for his actions and will admire the way in which you handled an unpleasant situation. If you have provoked the situation, he will also admire you for admitting your failure and correcting it. Either way, you are the winner!

Even if you do your part in going to him and the problem still is not solved, you must not discuss it with others. Even though you may have a King Saul for your boss, you still must respect his position and still honor him. Take your case before God and wait in faith for His vindication as Moses did in meekness.

The Inheritors

Whenever the word meekness is used in conversation today, we immediately draw the mental image of shyness and weakness. To be meek is to be weak, we think. So when Paul charged Titus (and all Christians) to "show all meekness unto all men" (Titus 3:2), we shake our heads in wonderment. Surely the Lord doesn't expect us to be meek (i.e., weak) as a mouse toward others.

The Greek word which is translated "meekness" is *prautes*, and it carries a much fuller, deeper significance than the common uses of its English counterpart. The following is the definition of *prautes* given in the *Expository Dictionary of New Testament Words* by W.E. Vine (New Jersey: Fleming H. Revell, n.d.)·

> *Prautes* (meekness) is an inwrought grace of the soul and the exercises of it are first and chiefly *toward God*. It is that temper of spirit *in which we accept His dealings with us as good and therefore without disputing or resisting*.
>
> This meekness, however, being first of all a meekness before God, is also such in the face of men, even of evil men, out of a sense that these, with the insults and injuries which they may inflict, are *permitted and employed by Him* for the chastening and purifying of His elect.
>
> It must be clearly understood therefore that the meekness manifested by the Lord and commended to the believer is the *fruit of power*. The common assumption is that when a man is meek, it is because he cannot help himself; but the Lord was "meek" *because* he had the infinite resources of God at His command. Described negatively, meekness is the opposite to self-assertiveness and self-interest; it is equanimity of spirit that is neither elated or cast down, simply *because it is not occupied with self at all*. (italics mine)

We need to fully understand what meekness really is, so that we can face people and circumstances with genuine meekness, not with an artificial attitude that comes when we think we must be colorless and bland in our responses. Meekness is ultimate trust in God as we face our circumstances, knowing that anything God wants us to face is fine with us; meekness is recognizing that circumstances are agents of God to correct and perfect; and meekness is the fruit of power. A person can be genuinely meek only when he realizes that all the power of the Godhead stands behind him. When he is attacked, therefore, he will not attempt to defend himself, because there is no need to. Notice too from the definition that the person who is meek is neither ecstatic over a good circumstance nor plunged into despair over bad circumstances. He is even-keeled and consistent, simply because circumstances either please or displease self, and he is not concerned with self.

One of the greatest examples of scriptural meekness was demonstrated in the life of Elisha, a fiery old prophet who was anything but timid and weak.

The king of Syria, on this occasion (2 Kings 6), had begun a campaign against Israel. In the secrecy of his tent, the king would call his counselors and captains together to map out the strategy to be used against Israel. But the king of Israel had a man whose abilities surpassed even those of Agent 007. Whenever the king of Syria decided on a tactic, such as an ambush or suprise attack, the Lord God of Israel would simply reveal the battle plan to Elisha, who would in turn relate it to the king of Israel. Syria was frustrated at every turn, its efforts completely nullified. The Scriptures say that "the heart of the king of Syria was sore troubled."

Calling his counselors together again, the king of Syria demanded to know who the traitor was. Someone, he logically concluded, must be giving Israel secret information or leaking the battle plans to the press. One of his servants replied, "None, my lord, O king: but Elisha, the prophet that is in Israel, telleth the king of Israel the words that thou speakest in thy bedchamber."

"So that's what's going on!" the King exclaimed. "I've

been foiled by a religious fanatic! Go and find out where this prophet is," he ordered.

Soon, word came back to the king that Elisha was in Dothan. That evening, the Syrian army was deployed around Dothan. Elisha could not possibly have escaped their grasp. Just before daylight, the trap was complete. Dothan was surrounded by a great host of armed soldiers, horses and chariots—all for one man. The general of the army smiles to himself, "Not even a mouse could escape without our notice. We've got their secret weapon now!"

As the sun was rising, Elisha and his servant, Gehazi, were just awaking. Gehazi went up on the roof of the house to wash his face, and as he glanced toward the horizon, he just about had a heart attack. In a circle around the city was the whole Syrian army. And he knew what they wanted—his master. He rushed back downstairs and breathlessly told Elisha that the city was surrounded. "Alas, master," he cried, "what shall we do?"

Elisha just smiled and patted Gehazi on the shoulder. "Fear not," he said, "for they that be with us are more than they that be with them."

Gehazi probably thought that his poor old master had prophesied his last prophecy and seen his last vision and was ready for the nursing home. But Elisha led Gehazi back to the roof and prayed, "Lord, I pray thee, open his eyes, that he may see."

"And the Lord opened the eyes of the young man and he saw: and behold, the mountain was full of horses and chariots of fire round about Elisha."

Then Elisha prayed again and the entire Syrian army was smitten with blindness by the Lord. Leaving the city, Elisha went forth and, after forming a human chain of his defeated foe, led the whole army captive to the king of Israel.

Examine Elisha's response to this circumstance, certainly

one we would consider disastrous, in light of the definition of scriptural meekness. Elisha recognized the hand of the Lord in this situation. He had full confidence that God had not slipped up and allowed the situation to get out of control. Elisha knew the Lord was in control, and accepted the circumstance.

Without even blinking an eye, Elisha told Gehazi that God had the situation well in hand and had sent His army to the rescue. Elisha knew the angelic army and fiery chariots were there all the time. He knew *any time* he needed the power of God, he had it at his disposal. When Gehazi told him the news, Elisha didn't have to go to his prayer closet; he didn't have to fall on his face and hope God would get him out of that mess.

And because Elisha had no concern for himself, he was not alarmed about the situation. Nor was he proud of what God was about to do for him.

We are to be fully confident in God's power backing us up, completely submitted to His will, and consistent in our faith, regardless of whether self is pleased or displeased by a circumstance. When the seventy disciples returned to Jesus with the good news that "even devils are subject to us in your name," Jesus replied, "Yes, but rejoice rather that your names are written in heaven." We know that Jesus must have been pleased at the disciples' discovery, but He already knew His power. The disciples were still spiritual children. He wanted them to mature to a steady, consistent faith in the power of His name. These seventy disciples later dwindled down to twelve, and then to zero as Christ faced the cross. We have spurts of enthusiasm, but then dive into despair because we have not learned spiritual meekness.

In the Sermon on the Mount, Jesus said, "Blessed are the meek, for they shall inherit the earth." Perhaps the Lord wants us to prepare for this great inheritance by learning, through meekness, to inherit the office. It is my firm conviction that He wants us to manifest the fruit of power in the face of personal attacks (as He himself did repeatedly). "Fear not, for they that be with us are more than they that be with them" (2 Kings 6:16).

When you are innocent of accusations, when you are faced with injustices because of your obedience to God's will, respond with meekness. Do not stop honoring the boss. Make "Remember King Saul!" your battle cry, knowing that God will vindicate and surround you with heavenly hosts, exalt and honor you as He did David. If you fail to honor your boss when he has proven himself to be your enemy, and yet at the same time try to practice meekness, you will be robbing Peter to pay Paul and you still will not be obedient to the whole will of God for the Christian at the office.

If you will honor your superiors in thought, word, and deed, regardless of the cost to you, control your tongue and develop a meek spirit, you will have become a truly unique person, one who stands secure in the eye of the storm.

CHAPTER NINE

The Crooked Path Made Straight

It's ten-thirty in the morning and Chuck is trying to work on a proposal—but he's really not trying very hard. He finally puts his pencil down and looks out the window. He begins to think about the man he met last week during a business appointment.

The man was the president of a large, successful company across town. The thing that has stuck in Chuck's mind is a comment the man made to him: "I wish all my men were as capable as you. Why don't you drop by to see me when you've got time to talk."

Ever since the meeting, Chuck has been thinking about that remark and wondering about the possibilities of leaving his present job. "Did Mr. Bennett really mean that?" Chuck thinks to himself. "I wonder if he would hire me. . . ." Chuck was flattered by the compliment. It was nice to have his abilities noticed. "I'm certainly not appreciated much around here," he thinks as he studies the building across the street. He sighs and returns to his work—for a moment.

He writes a few words and numbers, then examines his pencil again. "This is a good job," he thinks to himself. "I like it here, but I know for a fact that Bennett's company pays more than this one, and they get three weeks vacation. . . ." All of a sudden the door flies open and the boss storms in.

"How are you coming on that proposal?" he snaps. Chuck hops to and, for the next fifteen minutes, gives the boss his undivided attention. They discuss the report and arrive at several conclusions. But the moment the boss walks out of the door, Chuck is staring out the window again. "I like my boss," he says to himself, "even though he's been a little irritable lately. There's nothing wrong with this company—compared to most, I guess—but I wonder. . . ."

Here we have observed another very common symptom of the MMM Syndrome—the greener grass pattern. It's a problem as old as man himself. Abraham's nephew, Lot, looked around at Abraham's land, saw that the grass was greener in the distance and packed up to move near Sodom, which, incidentally, got him into a lot of trouble.

"But," some readers will object, "what has Chuck really done wrong? Different opportunities arise on many occasions. Aren't we supposed to want to better ourselves and look for ways to advance? If we pass up valuable opportunities, we may never get another chance. We have to look to the future and be prepared—we have families to think of, you know. Chuck was only thinking about the situation. . . ."

Let's explore the various aspects of Chuck's thinking.

From the Heart

Ephesians 6:5,6 reads: Servants, be obedient to them that are your masters according to the flesh, with fear and trembling, in singleness of your heart, as unto Christ; not with eyeservice, as menpleasers, but as the servants of Christ, doing the will of God from the heart.

As Chuck dreamed longingly about a job with the other company, what happened? He lost his singleness of heart. Thus it was difficult to keep his attention on the proposal he was supposed to work up. Furthermore, he violated the Scripture which commands us "whatsoever thy hand findeth to do, do it with *all thy might.*"

That's not all Chuck did wrong either. This Scripture in Ephesians mentions eyeservice. That refers to people who work only when the boss's eyes are upon them! Chuck certainly qualifies for that category of employee.

Look at the number of scriptural truths Chuck went against by just dreaming at his desk! Dreaming doesn't seem so bad, does it—until we compare it with the behavior God expects of us.

Daydreaming, always looking at—or for—the greener grass is not a light thing. A man who is constantly wondering about his employment is unsettled on and off the job. He has a constant question mark in his mind that robs him of satisfaction and contentment, not to mention robbing his company of his time and talent, for which he is, in good faith, being paid.

For the Christian, the most common cause of green-grassing is the attitude: "Although I have given myself totally to God, and have entrusted my future in His hands, I have to make the specific decisions on my own. God expects me to decide. . . ." What we really mean is: "God needs my help in planning my career. He's so busy that He might overlook a good opportunity for me!" So off we go mentally exploring the possibilities which appear on the horizon, carefully plotting, planning and scheming. And we do this in the face of the words of Christ, "Take no thought for the morrow."

Constantly wondering if we are employed in the right

place, in the job best suited to our talents and needs according to us, is unbelief.

God wants us to be fully reliant on Him in our employment. But there is another reason why we should not be constantly searching for an opportunity—that reason is our own need for contentment. Trust in God and contentment are so closely intertwined that we cannot separate them.

The Scriptures say, "The steps of a good man are ordered by the Lord," and "A man's heart deviseth his way, but the Lord directeth his steps." In these passages, we find assurance that God is fully directing our lives, every move we make. We also find a piece of advice—stop planning. We can devise all we want to, but God is directing. In other words, all our planning is in vain. It is an exercise in futility. If you are committed to God, He will lead you unerringly toward the goal that He has set for you.

Our sixth principle is, therefore:

YOU MUST TRUST THE LORD TO DIRECT YOUR CAREER

Had Chuck embraced and practiced this principle, his response to meeting the president of that other company would have been entirely different. In the first place, he would not have dwelt on the thought for a week (with no end in sight). His response to the situation would have been, "Lord, I thank you for bringing me into favor with him. I thank you for the opportunity that is before me; but Lord, I want to be employed only where you want me to be. I know you are directing my career and I commit the matter into your hands. If this is your will for me, open the door wide; if it is not, close the door completely."

You see, God is in the business of giving His children

definite guidance. But, by nature, we are in the business of guiding ourselves. With our earthly masters, we expect to be given assignments and orders. We expect instructions. We expect him to have control over our lives at the office. And we expect pay day also. We would think it was awfully strange if our superior told us, "Oh, just look around and see if you can find something to do with yourself." Yet we like to think that that's the very attitude God has. We should expect assignments and instructions from our heavenly master, just as surely as we expect them from earthly masters.

When we resign our willfulness and look to God to control our careers—and are confident that He will do it—we experience peace. If you trust God you must relinquish your right to guide your own career. Some people will say, "But I want to guide my own career. I have goals and ambitions I want to fulfill!" What a dangerous attitude. Nothing but frustration and storms await the man who holds to his desire to determine his own career. Remember the "old man"? "There is a way which seemeth right unto a man, but the end thereof are the ways of death."

But even those who have relinquished their rights to control their careers still worry because they aren't fully trusting God. We have a choice of attitudes. We can say, "God controls my career. I want His will for my life. He is able to guide and direct me unerringly, and therefore I don't have to be concerned about my career at all." Or we can say, "I know God controls my career. I know He will guide me if and when I change jobs . . . but I think I'll think (*worry*) about it in the meantime!" This is the source of daydreaming, double-mindedness, doing the will of God from the head, and performing our duties with only half our might.

If you trust the Lord to control your career, you must give

up worrying, green-grassing, daydreaming, and everything that interferes with your present job and that is causing you to look into the future, trying to figure out what will happen. Chuck, for example, had for all practical purposes simply walked out of the office and moved into an office at the other company.

When we trust God with the details of our employment, we can enter into a part of the Christian experience that few Christians ever see—the ultimate *rest*. It is described in Hebrews 4:9-10: "There remaineth therefore a rest to the people of God. For he that is entered into his rest, he also hath ceased from his own works, as God did from his."

Doesn't that sound wonderful? In the harried, hurried world of the office, isn't it wonderful to know that God has a rest available for you? That rest is a deep form of contentment; but it is available only to the children of God. To enter, however, even the Christian must cease from his labor, that hard, exhausting work of our own efforts. In this passage, Paul was talking about the Israelites, who wandered around the desert for forty years, because they did not trust God. They failed to enter into the rest that God had for them, because of unbelief. They could not turn control of their lives over to God and trust Him completely.

Psalm 23 echoes God's promise of rest. As the Good Shepherd, He leads us beside still waters and restores our souls. He does this for us for His own name's sake. The very name of God, His reputation, is at stake when you assume the name of Christian. You become a child of God and God becomes your Father, who is responsible for seeing that you are brought up properly! No father would say to his children, "Run along now, and fend for yourselves. I don't have any plans for you. I'm not going to provide for your needs or teach you how to live." No, a good father provides all the needs of his children, watches out for them all the time, and teaches them how to live. As Jesus said, "Then how much more will your heavenly Father give. . . ." When you accept the care and direction that your heavenly Father desires to give you, you enter into the rest of God.

Paul knew and experienced this rest of God. He wrote, "I have learned, in whatsoever state I am, therewith to be content." Whether dining with kings or supping with beggars, Paul was happy, content, and at rest.

One day, Paul and Silas cast a demon out of a young girl. As a result, they were beaten and thrown into prison. The girl had a spirit of divination and had made money for her masters by telling fortunes and soothsaying. But when this evil spirit left her at Paul's command, she lost her moneymaking ability. That made her masters angry. It was at their complaint that Paul and Silas were punished by beatings and imprisonment.

That first night, with their wounds still fresh, what do we find them doing? They were praising God. Praising God for what? For being their God, for using them to spread the gospel and . . . is it possible that they were praising Him for their wounds and for their predicament? Is it possible that they were praising God for their being in prison?

As Paul and Silas praised God, the earth shook violently for a moment and when the tremor stopped, the prison door stood wide open. Nothing was broken; the walls still stood; but the prison door was open.

Paul and Silas had a secret technique which gained them all those victories. Of course, we Christians don't have that much power today—do we? Do we know what secret weapon they had? It was simple trust in God, and that's all it was. But saying "just trust in God" is like saying "just set off a bomb!" Trust is powerful because God is powerful. Paul and Silas simply understood that all their circumstances were designed by God; that there were no peaks and valleys in

Christ; and therefore, they must be in prison because God had designed that circumstance. They were where God wanted them to be at that moment.

It has to be a dynamic experience to have God cause an earthquake just for you, just because you believe in His Son, and because He loves you and you love Him! I believe that if we had the kind of trust in God that Paul and Silas had, God would move in miraculous ways more and more often in our lives.

What does that kind of trust produce in your life? Contentment. As you submit to God in every situation in which you find yourself, contentment begins to flow from your heart and your life. Paul was not begging God to get him out of prison; he was not pitying himself; he wasn't rebuking the devil; he wasn't wondering if the prison across town had better accommodations; he was praising God for that particular situation. Paul was content even in prison.

This contentment doesn't just come to you. It doesn't come as a gift of the Holy Spirit during a good sermon or a fruitful prayer time. It comes by practice, by experience, by endurance, and by choosing to trust God. For this reason Paul said, "I have learned to be content. . . ." He learned it by having his own Christian brothers distrust him and run him out of town; he learned it when he was shipwrecked; he learned it when he was thrown into prison; he learned it by being beaten; he learned it when he faced trial for heresy; he learned it by enduring his thorn in the flesh.

A high goal of the Christian life is contentment. Contentment is a characteristic God wants us to have, and enjoy. We need to picture our lives as a maze. We cannot see which paths lead out and which ones lead to dead ends. If you have ever been inside a maze you know how frustrating it is to try to find your way out. Only God, knowing the end from the beginning, can see which paths we should take and which we should avoid.

God is able to open and close doors, to guide us specifically in our careers. Not long after I was converted to Christ, I found myself growing very bored with my job, although by all standards it was a good one. One day a friend of mine, Ron, told me of a position that had become available in an engineering company. He thought I might be interested. The more I thought about it, the better it looked. The location was in a state I had always liked and hoped to move to someday. The job offered a substantial raise in salary also, which my family and I needed. From all appearances, the job looked ideal.

I asked Ron to put in a good word for me with the company. A couple of weeks later, he informed me that the company was definitely interested and wanted to see my resume. After submitting one, I anxiously waited for the reply. One week went by, then two, then four. I called Ron on several occasions to see if he had heard anything, but he always assured me that the job was still open and that I was being given definite consideration.

As I nervously waited for a decision from the company, it finally occurred to me to pray. I asked the Lord to lead me and to lead the company in their decision. I asked God to open or close the door, whichever He wanted for me.

A few days later, I heard that the job had been filled. The company had selected another man. To be quite frank, I was a little put out with God for not letting me have that job. Didn't He know I was capable? Didn't He know how badly we needed that extra income? Didn't He know that I looked to Him for my career? But God was silent.

About a month later, I was shocked to learn that a tremendous upheaval had taken place in that company I had wanted to join. Many people, including the man who was selected instead of me, and his boss, were fired. Because of a serious recession in the business, many people lost their jobs, and had I been selected for a job, I would have been one of them. I praised God for protecting me, and asked forgiveness for my unbelief. Some months later, I learned that the company had gone bankrupt. Only then did I realize the extent to which God had directed my life.

You can imagine my relief. I thanked God time and again for protecting me and my family. And God gently reminded me of the time I had spent worrying and fretting—and doubting His concern when I didn't get the job. I had given Him my life, and I believed that He loved me and was directing me for my good. Yet when He handed down His decision to me, I wasn't so sure—for a while. That incident had a tremendous impact on my attitude toward my career.

Another important truth I learned was one that all new Christians should learn, and the sooner the better. Paul saw the effects of the Holy Spirit working in the lives of new believers, then as now, and saw the zeal and excitement produced. And as a result, those people often stepped out in faith into a ministry, just as some people do today.

When God begins to move miraculously through a believer to meet the needs of others, the new believer so often thinks he has been called into a full-time Christian ministry, because of the anointing from God on their lives. They quit their jobs to study for the ministry or to become evangelists. Unfortunately, years later, they find themselves in despair, disappointment, and failure. God can redeem the failure, but those people have missed God's will for all those years. From Paul's experience of witnessing the same thing in the lives of early Christians, he wrote to the church in Corinth (which was somewhat notorious for its enthusiasm anyway):

Let every man abide in the same calling wherein he was called. Art thou called being a servant? care

> not for it: but if thou mayest be made free, use it
> rather. For he that is called in the Lord, being a
> servant, is the Lord's freeman: likewise also he
> that is called, being free, is Christ's servant. Ye are
> bought with a price; be not ye the servants of men.
> Brethren, let every man, wherein he is called,
> therein abide with God. (1 Cor. 7:20-24)

We can ask, Are you a lawyer? Are you a teacher? Are you a
banker? Whatever you were doing when you came to the
Lord, continue in that profession.

Paul uses the word "calling" in two ways. The first use
means God's calling you to become a Christian. But the
second use means your career, your line of work, or your
occupation. Your job, according to Paul's usage of the word,
is your calling. Today, we have narrowed the term "calling"
to a person's decision to go into the ministry, but according
to the Scriptures, your profession is your calling.

Notice, too, that Paul writes, "Let every man wherein he
is called therein abide with God." Were you a newspaper
reporter when you were called into the kingdom of God?
Now you are a newspaper reporter with God. Were you a
doctor when you came to the Lord? Now you are a doctor
with God. Do you see the significance of the one small
phrase, "with God"? Being with the almighty God as you go
about your daily routine should make a tremendous
difference in your job.

We like to encourage young men to become pastors. We
feel that this is more spiritual or more pleasing to God than
secular work. Many churches consider it a feather in their
caps to be able to boast of having produced six ministers,
four music directors and two education directors—not to
mention the two ministerial students who will be graduating
next year. This attitude, that full-time Christian work is

somehow the only spiritual occupation, is entirely unscriptural. Truly, people are called by God into the ministry; but people are also called by God into all professions. You will probably never hear anyone say, "Praise God! I've been called into banking!" or "I've been called into marketing!" or "The Lord has called me into laboratory research!" Yet they have been called into those professions.

The Word of God makes no distinction between the full-time Christian worker and the Christian laity. Every Christian is in full-time Christian work, regardless of what job they perform Monday through Friday. You are either born again or you're not. You are either a disciple of Christ or you're not. God is touching the lives of people in every walk of life. He is not so interested in occupations as He is in people, and all gainful employment, all fields of endeavor (with the exception of a few jobs which involve morally questionable practices) are pleasing to Him. Every Christian should tell himself—until he knows it—"my work is pleasing to God—I'm a full-time Christian, so my job is a full-time Christian ministry!"

We are experiencing a fresh outpouring of the Holy Spirit around the world today, and we are not accustomed to having ordinary Christian men and women spearheading evangelism. The world can't get used to the idea that the strength of evangelism and person-to-person witnessing is coming not only from ministers but from businessmen and housewives, as well as the next-door neighbor and the shopkeeper down the street. If you witnessed to a construction worker fifteen or even ten years ago, he was likely to respond, "What are you—a preacher?" Not any more. The ordinary Christian has gotten in on the world-wide harvesting!

Because of the vast numbers of people coming into the

kingdom and the fresh work of the Holy Spirit in lives today, we have a great rush of people going out on faith. When a Christian shares or ministers to a group of people about something God has done and shown him, people inevitably come up to him afterward and say, "Brother, God is calling you to preach!" or "Brother, you ought to go into the ministry." He already has. He's ministering, isn't he? This concept of the ministry and full-time Christian work is wrong, because we are all called to preach and minister. Jesus told his disciples—a fisherman, a tax collector and the like—to preach the gospel. Preaching means simply to proclaim; we have all been called to proclaim the gospel.

Throughout his life, Paul remained a tentmaker. In his letters, he wrote, "I worked to earn my own living while I was with you. I did not ask you to support me. I was not a burden to you when I stayed with you. I earned my own keep." He also wrote, "Let him who once was a thief, turn to honest labor with his hands"; and he ordered, "if any will not work, neither shall he eat."

You see, work is an important discipline. Paul knew if a man could not be responsible enough to hold steady employment, then he was not fit for the service of God. Refusal to work always reflects a lack of discipline, an immaturity, and sometimes sheer laziness. Without the discipline of work, a man is not equipped to work in the spiritual realm, because that person has shown himself to be unmoldable and unteachable. Furthermore, God isn't likely to want people who can't make it in the secular world of employment to go into Christian-related jobs.

First Timothy 6:6 reads: "Godliness with contentment is great gain." You cannot be godly until you are content. And you cannot be content until you fully trust God. What is contentment? It is *not* a feeling of ecstasy over your work. It is God-given satisfaction; it is saying "All is well with my soul." It is the firm knowledge that "God is my Father; what more do I need?"

Contentment is also perfect agreement with God. The Scriptures ask, "Can two walk together unless they be agreed?" Can you walk with God unless you *agree* with Him, agree to His purposes, and agree with His principles? No. Contentment comes from agreeing with God, with His purposes, His plans for your life, and with His principles and truths. Just as we cannot imagine the Father and the Son having bad moods and fluctuations in their personalities, neither can we imagine them having arguments. It is absolutely absurd to try to picture an argument in heaven between the three persons of the Godhead. The Father, the Son, and the Holy Spirit are in perfect agreement all the time. When we come to the point in our lives that we are content all the time, it is because we agree with God at every moment, with every circumstance, and in every state. This kind of agreement, which is really submission, must precede godliness. When we agree with God, peace begins to flow like a river. We become pliable in the hands of God. Godliness is then produced in us by Him. God and God alone can produce godliness, by His own nature working in us. If we lack contentment, which means we lack trust and submissiveness, then we are constantly pulling at the bit. There is a constant questioning, a never-ending tug of war about the affairs of our lives.

Such mental tension robs us of effectiveness in our jobs, of peace in our circumstances and of spiritual growth. In studying the life of Joseph, we saw that he was content to prosper wherever he was. He prospered by diligence in Potiphar's household; he prospered in prison; he prospered as ruler over Egypt. God has placed you in your present job for a purpose. You could be gaining valuable experience which will prepare you for what God has planned for you later; you could be learning spiritual lessons at the hand of your boss and co-workers. Whatever the purpose God has for your present job, you must learn to be content in that situation.

We have all seen job-hoppers, and the consequences of their constant job changing is sad. A person's employment record is suspicious when his resume reads that he has had five jobs in the past three years and the reason for leaving each was "I didn't like my work," or something of that nature. Most of the time, job-hoppers are trying to find Shangri-la.

Picture two men in offices across the street from each other. Frank looks out the window into Dan's office. "Boy," he thinks, "just look at that! He sure does have a nice office; all the plush carpeting. His company just had a full-page ad in all the papers—they must be really bringing in the money. Here I sit in this shabby office, and I have to stand on my head just to get supplies. Heaven only knows when I'll get a raise. . . ."

Dan, who has been furiously working under a great deal of pressure, looks out the window to the office across the street, just as Frank has gotten up to get a cup of coffee.

"I tell you," Dan says to himself, "that guy's got it made. He's sitting there drinking coffee and reading the paper. I sure do wish I had that kind of job. I'm going to get ulcers from this place. It's a slave factory . . . push, push, push. . . ."

Discontent is like a cancer, it keeps eating away unless you cut it out. The plumber wants to be an electrician, the electrician wants to be an insurance salesman, the salesman wants to be a lawyer, the lawyer wants to be a congressman and the congressman wants to be president. And probably, none of them dislike their jobs; it's just that discontent is working in their inner man like poison. The grass always does look greener on the other side, because we view the grass from a distance. We see in the distance a hill of luxurious grass and we head for it. But when we reach the top of that hill and look down at the grass, we can see weeds and dirt and bare spots. "Why," we exclaim, "it's just like the grass I was on before!" From a distance, we couldn't see the flaws, only the green carpet of grass.

Searching for the ideal jobs, like searching for the ideal set of circumstances, is futile. Solomon, who searched for the supreme happiness in life, wrote "vanity of vanities," after each search. The book of Ecclesiastes portrays the unregenerate heart, the natural man, and deals with the different courses of action available to man, all the searches he makes. Many people who continually long and look for a better job and lot in life are really searching for God, and they, too, sigh "vanity of vanities" as each accomplishment leaves them disappointed. For the man whose life is empty and meaningless, work seems to be the best scapegoat, the culprit. Even Christians blame their lack of peace and joy on their jobs. But a new and better job will never heal anyone's discontent.

The principle of trusting God fully, which results in contentment, is built upon the previous principles. If God controls the company, employs you, holds the future, designs your circumstances, and is your actual employer, then you can trust Him with your present work situation and your future ones, the entire course of your career. God put you where you are now, even if you weren't aware of God's leading at the time. Every time you start looking at all the green grass across the street, say to yourself, "I know God put me in this place, and I won't leave until He leads me to make a move. I will be content, knowing that my heavenly Father is directing me every step of the way." If you can trust God with your entire future, you can surely trust Him to let you know if and when to change jobs. He is able to specifically lead you, by circumstances He has designed, by the inner witness of the Holy Spirit, and by His Word. He is able to do this, and you can and must depend upon it.

"There remaineth therefore a rest to the people of God. For he that is entered into his rest, he also hath ceased from his own works, as God did from his" (Heb. 4:9-10).

CHAPTER TEN

The Reward of the Righteous

The final symptom of the MMM Syndrome is the recurring fever which accompanies the grasping desire for status. We are all acutely aware of the status symbols awarded in the business world. As one moves through the hierarchy of a company, like climbing the rungs of a ladder, each higher level of management has advantages over the previous one—in a deliberate and well-planned pattern. Each office is a little larger and more elaborate than the one just below it. The president's office, of course, is largest of all, complete with a massive desk, original paintings, a wet bar, beautiful furniture, and a private bath. The symbols, which define our status to the world, do not by any means stop at the office decor, however.

Upon being promoted to assistant vice-president, Larry suddenly realizes that the Chevy Impala is getting a little old. Funny, he thinks, that he didn't notice what bad shape it was in before. Suddenly, his clothes seem worn, his house seems too small, and his furniture too shabby. After all, he must look and live in a manner worthy of his high position. He has his eye on the country club, private schools for children; boats; vacations in the Bahamas—and his wife has always dreamed of a trip to Europe. Even the church membership could stand some adjustment to fit this new job. Every aspect of his life is touched by the promotion.

The Scriptures have quite a lot to say about status, and about that substance which supposedly brings it—money. Much of what the Bible says about money, however, is difficult to understand and at times appears somewhat contradictory. On one hand, we are told not to lay up treasures, and on the other hand, we are encouraged to make friends of unrighteous mammon.

Furthermore, the most often-quoted text about money muddles the picture even more. Jesus' words to the rich young ruler have been used extensively to denounce material wealth and to promote tithing and charity. Jesus' words were: "Sell all that you have and give the money to the poor." Yet John wrote, "Brethren, I would that you prosper, even as your soul prospers." And God does not seem to have anything against His servants having wealth, since the list of great men of the Old Testament reads like a list of "The Ten Richest Men of Israel." The result for the modern Christian is confusion.

What Else Should I Do?

Let's look more closely at the story of the rich young ruler (Matt. 19:16-30) who came to Jesus for advice to gain insight into the matter of material possessions in the Christian life.

The young man approached Jesus one day and asked, "Master, what must I do to have eternal life?" Jesus replied, "Keep the commandments of God."

"But which commandment," the young man asked, "is the most important?" Jesus quoted several commandments to him, stressing most the importance of loving God and loving your neighbor.

"All these things have I done since I was a child!" the young man answered, somewhat exasperated. "What else should I do?"

The young ruler continued to press for answers. When Christ told him what the most important commandments were, the young man did not, as would be expected, respond, "Well, thank you for telling me; I'm in good shape then, because I have kept these commandments all my life," and walk off with a sigh of relief. The young man knew that something further was needed to gain eternal life. He had a void that he could not fill, so he continued to question the Master until he got his answer.

When the young man asked the third question, Jesus answered this time, "Go and sell all that you have and give the money to the poor." Look at what the young man did then—he hung his head in sorrow and walked away. Jesus had put His finger on the problem. When the young man was not satisfied that he had done all that he should in life, Christ identified his weakness.

In Christ's first answer to the ruler, to obey the commandments, especially the first two, He was giving the general will of God for every person. But His answer to the young man about his great wealth addressed the need of that particular man. Christ had touched the sore spot in the man's life. In his case, he did not possess his wealth; his wealth possessed him. He knew that something was wrong and that something more was required from him by God. He sensed that something was amiss in his heart, but he didn't know what it was. Christ's answer to sell all he had was exactly what that young man needed to do, as evidenced by the fact that he hung his head and turned away in sorrow—that was the one thing he didn't want to do. Jesus' command was extreme because the young man's problem was extreme. Nothing less than selling all, cutting himself away from his treasure, would heal the young man's heart.

When the young ruler walked away, Jesus turned to his disciples and said, "It is easier for a camel to go through the eye of a needle than for a rich man to enter into the kingdom of God."

Jesus often used common everyday situations that arose to illustrate a spiritual principle. In those days, cities were surrounded by high walls for protection. At nightfall, the gates of the city were closed and barred until sunrise the next morning. Once the gates were locked, they were opened for no one. But just to the side of the main gate was a very small opening in the wall for latecomers, citizens or travelers who didn't make it in before closing time. The late arriver would dismount his camel, unload the baggage, and make the beast crawl through the small tunnel-like opening. Then the man would himself, carrying his baggage, crawl through. The tunnel was just large enough to allow the man and camel, one at a time, but completely effective in keeping out an army. Because of the size of the tunnel, it became known as "the eye of the needle" (Bob Mumford, *The King and You* [New Jersey: Fleming H. Revell, 1974], p. 207).

Jesus was saying to His disciples that it is harder for a rich man to enter the kingdom of God than it was for a camel to squeeze through the tunnel in the wall. In order to enter the city of heaven, we must pass through a spiritual eye of the needle. But we cannot if we are loaded down. Like the camel, we must have every piece of baggage lifted from us because in the eye of the needle there is only room for you—and your Master, Christ.

This was the young ruler's problem. He was loaded down. He could not fit through the eye of the needle to enter into eternal life. Jesus instructed us not to lay up treasures on earth—"for where your treasure is, there will your heart be also." The rich young ruler had kept all the commandments, but his heart was not in it. Your heart cannot be in two places at once. The young ruler's wealth was a great weight to him, and Jesus therefore told him that he needed his burden removed. Christ's answer to him was not harsh or punitive—it was merciful and truthful. The man had to let go of his treasure so he could take the hand of his Master—which he would not do.

The disciples marveled at Jesus' answer to the man. "If it is so hard for a rich man to enter the kingdom of God, then how can any person with any wealth at all be saved?" the disciples asked incredulously. Jesus answered, "With men, this is impossible; but with God all things are possible." In other words, man alone cannot lift his burdens off, no more than the camel can remove his own baggage. Only Christ, the Master, can remove the burdens.

The Apostle Paul echoed the same principle when he said, "Lay aside every weight and sin, which so easily besets us and run with patience the race. . . ." Weight and sin are different problems. Material possessions, money, and prestige are weights, not sins. Jesus did not speak to the rich young ruler about his sin, for he had kept all the commandments, and had loved God all his life. His problem was not sin, but weight. In contrast, however, Jesus spoke to the woman caught in adultery about her sin, not her weights. He told her to go and sin no more. He didn't tell her to go and sell all her possessions; nor did He tell the ruler to go and sin no more.

This distinction between weights and sins is important to our understanding God's attitude toward money. Let's look at an example of a burdensome financial weight.

Jerry has been a Christian for five years. He and his family have been active in all phases of church activities and in the past year he was chosen to teach an adult Sunday school class. Jerry, having pretty successfully integrated his faith and his life style, is contented and has developed a sense of self-worth through being used by God to help others at work and at the church.

During these years as a Christian, God blessed Jerry financially. Raises and promotions came steadily and now, for the first time, Jerry is out of debt. There is extra money left over after all the bills are paid each month and now he and his family can enjoy some of those things that they have always wanted. Since Jerry loved fishing and water skiing, he saved up enough money to purchase a boat.

Soon after the boat was brought home, Jerry and his son were enjoying those Saturday afternoon fishing trips; the whole family learned how to ski and often all of Saturday and Sunday afternoons were spent at the lake, fishing, picnicking, and skiing.

After several highly enjoyable months of weekends with the boat, Jerry's wife began to notice that her husband was irritable and grouchy. When she asked him about it, Jerry replied, "I just don't seem to have enough time any more; there's always something breaking down around the house that I've got to fix. The yard looks terrible and needs a lot of work—but I just don't have time. I always feel pressured for time as it is. . . ."

After Sunday school class a couple of weeks later, Jerry happened to overhear one of the members of his class commenting as he walked out the door, "I don't know why, but the lessons just don't seem to be as good as they used to be."

Jerry was hurt and resentful. He hadn't realized that the quality of his lessons had dropped off; but his class did. He hadn't realized that his quality as a husband and father had fallen; but his family did. Why?

Before Jerry had purchased the boat, he had ample time on weekends to keep up with home maintenance and prayerful preparation of his Sunday school material. In addition, he still had time for some recreation and other things he needed to do. But after obtaining the boat, the weekends were taken up on the lake and things had begun to pile up on him. He allowed the boat to consume his energy and time. As a result, his family and his class—and perhaps mostly he himself—had suffered. That boat had become a *weight* on him and had hindered his Christian walk. It weighed him down, keeping him from running the Christian race successfully.

Jerry had forgotten that the essence of the abundant life is service to others. He had allowed the priority of his time to gradually shift from that principle of service to the boat, a self-serving expenditure of time.

God doesn't mind our enjoying such things as boating, fishing, golf, and tennis, but He repeatedly warns us not to allow these blessings to become the top priorities in our lives. We cannot allow them to become weights to us, or we will soon find ourselves grinding to a halt in the Christian race. If Jerry doesn't realize his predicament, his weight will soon destroy his Christian witness entirely.

Seek Ye First

God did not say "Money is the root of all evil." We have heard this misquotation for generations. What God did say was, "The love of money is the root of all evil." When money becomes the prime object of your love, then and only then is money dangerous and evil for you. And the object of your love, the most important thing in your life, is that thing or person your whole being revolves around—your personality, your time, your energies. Your heart is with that object of your love.

Jesus spoke of our treasures. He warned us that where our treasure is, there will be our heart also. But He further told us to lay up treasures in heaven, where moths, rust, and thieves don't exist. So then, treasure has a much broader meaning than simply money. Webster defines "treasure" as "wealth of any kind or in any form; something of great worth or value." A treasure is anything that is precious to you, anything that you consider of great worth or value. The Bible speaks repeatedly of the riches and treasures of God, and these are the treasures to which Christ referred when He told us to store up treasures in heaven. God's treasures are the only ones that have lasting value. It all comes down to the fact that God doesn't want us to waste our lives spinning our wheels in pursuit of wealth that we cannot take with us when we die. A man cannot stand before God at the Judgment Seat and say, "Well, I have $50,000 in my bank account back home; my home is assessed, incidentally, at $80,000; and I left my wife a Cadillac to drive." God will answer, "No, John, that's not what I meant when I asked about your treasure. What treasure do you have up here?" If, when the angels audit your account with the First Universal Bank of Heaven, they find a balance of zero, it's all over!

Jesus said, "Seek ye first the kingdom of God and his righteousness, and all these things will be added unto you." The things to which He referred were food, clothing, and shelter, all the necessities of life that the disciples were worrying about. Jesus explained, "Take no thought for tomorrow, what ye shall wear and what ye shall eat, for your heavenly Father knows that ye have need of these things." Then Jesus gave us the promise that the Father would supply our needs, if we seek first the kingdom of God. We have heard the expression, "The way to a man's heart is through his stomach," and there is a great deal of truth to that! God's prime goal for His children is to generate complete dependence on Him. God can and does use man's need for material possessions and food—his stomach—to get to his heart, by either supplying the needs or withholding the provision.

Christ promised that "all these things would be added unto you"; but the requirement was first that you seek Him and His righteousness. Throughout the Scriptures, God has given first the promise, then the requirement. In speaking to the children of Israel who have just come out of Egypt, God promises them the land of Canaan; He tells them what He will do for them. They will eat the good of the land, live in houses they did not build, enjoy the vineyards they did not plant. He tells them it is a land of "brooks of water, of fountains and depths that spring out of valleys and hills; a land of wheat, and barley and vines and fig trees and pomegranates; a land of oil, olives and honey." God goes on to further describe the new land. But then comes the condition, a warning they must heed if they are to keep the promised land:

> Beware that thou forget not the Lord thy God, in not keeping his commandments, and his judgments, and his statutes, which I command thee this day: Lest when thou hast eaten and art full, and hast built goodly houses and dwelt therein; and when thy herds and thy flocks multiply, and thy silver and thy gold is multiplied; and all that thou hast is multiplied; Then thine heart be lifted up, and thou forget the Lord thy God. (Deut. 8:11-14)

God's warning was justified. Whenever the children of Israel were well-fed and secure, safe from enemies, they forgot the Lord their God and went merrily on their way—to idolatry. But when they faced an emergency, they cried out to God for forgiveness and help. When God answered their prayers and diverted the disaster, they went right back to their old ways. Christians today do the same thing. God wants us to mature to the place that we always love Him and follow Him, regardless of material provisions. This is why Jesus said, "Seek ye first the kingdom of God and his righteousness." If we do both, then we will be consistent in our love for God. Our top priorities should be two-fold: God's kingdom (His will) and God's righteousness (His ways). We should not seek one without the other. We should not simply get saved without going on to learn God's ways and principles; neither should we try to know God's ways without coming into the kingdom, via a vital relationship with Christ and his body. When both requirements are met, then God will provide your needs.

Christ promised us the necessities of life—not the luxuries of life. James wrote that "ye have not because ye ask not; ye ask, and receive not, because ye ask amiss, that ye may consume it upon your lusts." We cannot ask God to give us luxuries just to fulfill a need of the ego. God will not give us Cadillacs if we want them for pride. God will not give us a mansion, just so we can show off, or prove something to other people. Christ promised us clothes, food and shelter, all the necessities to sustain life. We have perhaps more necessities today—we must have transportation to go to work and enough money to send our children to school, but these are all included in "all these things will be added. . . ." God will supply our needs, not our wants.

God wants to bless us. God wants to shower us with good things. But so many Christians, like Jerry, turn a blessing into a weight, and sometimes even into a sin. God doesn't want anything in our lives to take the place that He and He alone should occupy. If you draw your security from material wealth, devote your energies to obtaining and maintaining wealth, and your material possessions are foremost in your thoughts, then they have taken the place of God in your heart. God is no longer your source, but your job has become your source. Your security comes no longer from God, but from your income and bank account. And God has a way of taking these things away from us. He doesn't do this to hurt or disappoint us, but to replace them with himself. When that is accomplished, He will return those things to you, as things, not as gods. When He has adjusted your perspective, your priorities, He will return unto you material possessions. So much depends upon your priorities in life.

In Ecclesiastes 5:18, Solomon wrote: "Behold that which I have seen: it is good and comely for one to eat and to drink, and to enjoy the good of all his labour that he taketh under the sun all the days of his life, which God giveth him: for it is his portion." It is good that man should enjoy the fruit of his labor. The next verse reads, "Every man also to whom God hath given riches and wealth, and hath given him power to eat thereof, and to take his portion, and to rejoice in his labour; this is the gift of God." Material blessings come from God only. As God continued His warning to the children of Israel, He admonished them to guard against conceit. "Lest thou forget the Lord thy God . . . And thou say in thine heart, My power and the might of mine hand hath gotten me this wealth. But thou shalt remember the Lord thy God: for it is he that giveth thee power to get wealth . . ." (Deut.

8:17-18). I know of a man who thought that his own abilities had gained him his wealth. When a needy woman came to him on one occasion, he gave her a large sum of money. But when the woman responded, "Oh, I thank God for this!" the man replied, "Don't thank God. I'm the one who did it."

Jesus told the story of a wealthy businessman who forgot the Lord his God. This man had accumulated such great wealth that he planned to expand his business. He decided to build bigger and better storehouses. He was very pleased with himself for his business acumen and the security of wealth he had now. "And I will say to my soul, Soul, thou hast much goods laid up for many years; take thine ease, eat, drink and be merry." But God said to him at that moment: "Thou fool, this night thy soul shall be required of thee: then whose shall those things be, which thou hast provided?"

When Jesus finished the story He said: "So is he that layeth up treasure for himself and is not rich toward God." The problem with the rich man was not his wealth per se, but his failure to accumulate riches in heaven. He had no good deeds to others; he had not given to the poor; he was like the rich man who would not help Lazarus. Jesus diagnoses the man's sin, therefore, as twofold: (1) he had accumulated wealth for himself and (2) he had neglected God. He was spiritually bankrupt. He had zero in the First Universal Bank of Heaven.

Though He Were Rich

Paul wrote, "Ye know the grace of our Lord Jesus Christ, that though he were rich, yet for your sakes, he became poor, that ye through his poverty might be rich." At the cross, a divine exchange occurred. When Christ left heaven to be born on earth, He left also all the wealth, riches, and glory of the universe to become penniless, and by our standards today, even destitute. He took off His crown and laid aside

His power and glory. Therefore, as He prayed in the Garden of Gethsemane before the crucifixion, He said, "I have glorified thee on earth: I have finished the work which thou gavest me to do. And now, O Father, glorify thou me with thine own self, with the glory which I had with thee before the world was." Christ was about to return to the Father and to be restored unto all the glory He had given up.

Because of the works and atonement of Christ, we who believe in Him can partake of the divine exchange—our sin for His righteousness; our poverty for His wealth; our human nature for His divine nature. Paul was writing primarily of the spiritual exchange that occurs when we are born again, but not exclusively. The divine exchange involves the whole man and extends to every aspect of our natures and lives. Through the poverty of Christ, we can become rich. Is God really interested in money? No. Is God interested in meeting our needs? Of course. God is indirectly interested in money, because He is directly interested in us.

What is the right attitude toward wealth? The right attitude is "it doesn't matter!" It is the attitude, "Lord, I will love you and follow you in the face of plenty and in the face of deprivation." So often we pray something like this: "Lord, if you will do this for me, then I will love you. . . ." It is the if-then attitude that God considers unhealthy in us. God has the right to use if-thens on us, but we do not have the right to use them on Him. We try to bargain with our love for God and our obedience to God, and these are not open to spiritual negotiation. If the attitude of the heart toward money is right, God can bless us materially without our taking our attention off Him and putting it on the blessings. We can accept a Cadillac on one hand and a mansion on the other and we will never move our eyes away from Him. We can also lose a Cadillac and a mansion and never even blink an eye, because it won't matter. We will say with Job, "The Lord giveth, the Lord taketh away, blessed be the name of the Lord." Our relationship with God won't be affected at all. On the other hand, if a Cadillac rolls in, and we sort of roll with it, and let that fine upholstery and powerful engine take the place of God in our hearts, then watch out. Even something like a nice pair of shoes or a new suit can infect our hearts with pride and turn our focus away from God. If our motivation is to "keep up with the Joneses," to fulfill the whims of the ego, or any other carnal motive, then the perspective of material possessions is out of focus and God must deal with the deficiency.

When Solomon became king of Israel, the Lord spoke to him one night and invited him to ask anything he wanted and it would be granted. Listen to Solomon's answer to God: "O Lord, . . . I am but a little child: I know not how to go out or come in. And thy servant is in the midst of thy people, which thou hast chosen; a great people, that cannot be numbered nor counted for multitude. Give, therefore, thy servant an understanding heart to judge thy people, that I may discern between good and bad; for who is able to judge this thy so great a people?" (1 Kings 3:7-9).

Solomon wanted wisdom, for the sake of God's people. He wanted supernatural wisdom so that he could do God's will. What was God's response? "And the speech pleased the Lord; that Solomon had asked this thing. And God said unto him, because thou hast asked this thing, and hast not asked for thyself long life; neither hast thou asked riches for thyself; nor hast asked the life of thine enemies, but hast asked for thyself understanding to discern judgment; Behold, I have done according to thy words; lo, I have given thee a wise and understanding heart; so that there was none like thee before thee neither shall any arise like unto thee."

But God didn't stop there. "And I have also given thee that which thou hast not asked, both riches and honor, so that there shall not be any among the kings like unto thee all thy days. And, if thou wilt walk in my ways, to keep my commandments, as thy father David did walk, then I will lengthen thy days" (1 Kings 3:10-14).

Solomon had his priorities right and God was pleased with him. Solomon could have asked for anything in the world, and gotten it—God had already promised to grant any request. In a theocracy as strong as Israel's, ruling God's people properly was a matter of administering the divine laws carefully. The king had to be both ruler and priest, theologian, and lawyer. Solomon wanted to fulfill his duties according to God's Word, but he realized his own inadequacies, and this, too, pleased God. God gave him not only what he asked for, but also everything he hadn't asked for as a bonus. Notice that the last thing God granted to Solomon was another "if-then." If Solomon would walk in the ways of God personally, as well as minister God's ways nationally, then God would give him long life.

Throughout the Bible, we find examples of God blessing His children with material blessings. Of Abraham, God actually made a great nation. To Job, God returned everything—sons, daughters (the most beautiful in the land), oxen, cattle, sheep, houses, and health—two times over what he had originally. Solomon, David, Joseph, and many others became very wealthy. Yet we Christians in recent centuries have had a secret guilt if God blessed us.

No doubt many rich young rulers have come to the knowledge of Christ and have turned their backs on wealth, and rightly so; no doubt God has called many people to give up all possessions to serve the poor. Yet the belief that poverty automatically equals spirituality is unscriptural. Many are the testimonies of men who suffered through the Depression in incredible lack, or endured some other calamity, only to find that as they followed the Lord, He led them to financial success, and sometimes great wealth. I know of one man who survived the Depression only because of bread lines. He tells that each morning before work, he would get soup in the bread lines and that was his only meal of the day. On weekends, he would just stay in bed because he was too weak to do anything except struggle down to the bread line. Until his retirement a few years ago, that man was chairman of the board of a large chain of prosperous department stores, and he is still a wealthy man. His testimony is that God alone is responsible for his success.

The irony of the fact that we are sometimes a little embarrassed by wealth is that we at the same time long—even lust—for wealth. God wants to adjust these attitudes. Proper priorities, like Solomon's, will free God's hand to bless you materially.

Jesus gave us the Lord's prayer to emphasize the vital relationship we are to have with Him, a relationship so alive that we don't even have to think about tomorrow. You may feel strange praying, "Father, give us this day our daily bread," when you know perfectly well that the cupboards and the freezer are stocked full of food, but rest in the assurance that God has indeed given you that provision. And know for a certainty that He is able to empty those cupboards in a hurry. It is significant that Jesus told us to pray for daily bread. We are to pray for provision day by day, not week by week or month by month. One aspect of the rich businessman's sin of storing up wealth for himself was that he drew his security from his wealth. He planned to build bigger barns, thinking that he would thus be wealthy and well-fed for years and years. He felt that he had insured his future.

Your top priority in life must be the kingdom of God and His righteousness. This is the only requirement for success in life. Our final principle is, therefore:

YOUR STATUS SYMBOL MUST BE THE CROSS, NOT THE DOLLAR

The only weight we are to feel on our backs is the weight of the cross. To non-Christians trying to decide upon an answer to life's questions, the cross appears to be too heavy. In reality, it is not nearly as heavy as the dollar we spend our whole lives trying to obtain. The cross is light and the burden is easy, and the rewards are great. The cross should be the only status symbol, the only mark of prestige we seek. God elevated Jesus to "the name above every name" and He wants to elevate us because we bear His name.

As Peter watched the rich young ruler walk away, he thought of the wealth the young man must have possessed. He pondered the instructions the young man received from Christ to sell all he had and give the money to the poor. He thought of his own situation. Turning to Jesus, Peter asked, "Master, we have left all and have followed thee." In other words, Peter was saying, "Lord, we have given up all, just as you advised the young ruler."

Jesus answered: "Verily I say unto you, There is no man that hath left house, or brethren, or sisters, or father, or mother, or wife, or children, or lands, for my sake, and the gospel's, but that he shall receive an hundredfold now in this time, houses, and brethren, and sisters, and mothers, and children, and lands, with persecutions; and in the world to come eternal life" (Mark 10:29-30).

Jesus offered us two rewards, one for the present life, and one for the afterlife, when we give up all to follow Him. In this life, we will receive an hundredfold more than what we gave up for Him. He said "with persecution" because we will always be persecuted when we receive what God has for us. The reward in the afterlife is eternal life. God's greatest gift to His children is the gift of eternal life, available only through belief in His Son, Jesus. Yet God does not want us to sit out our lives waiting for heaven, so He offers us rewards in this life also.

God can replace the fever for status and possessions with a burning desire to do only the will of God. When opportunities for advancement and promotion, for greater material wealth, come your way, you will think first, as your top priority, "Lord, I want to be in the center of your will. The money is not important to me." He will reward you for putting Him first in your life. But whatever riches He gives to you will be incidental, compared to His riches in glory.

CHAPTER ELEVEN

Proving the Foundation

We have now completed seven precepts concerning our occupations, each built upon the previous one. These precepts or principles are to become a part of the construction Jesus is performing in our lives, building us into His image. These principles will provide the foundation to support us at our places of employment, if we will allow them to take root in our hearts. In summary, the principles are:

1. God controls kingdoms and companies.
2. You are employed by Christ, not by your company.
3. Your future depends upon God and your response to Him.
4. Your circumstances are designed by God.
5. Count your superiors worthy in thought, word, and deed.
6. You must trust the Lord to direct your career.
7. Your only status symbol must be the cross.

As we attempt to integrate these principles into our lives, each one must be tested. When Jesus compared the house built upon a rock to the house built on sand, He said, "when the storms come," not "if the storms come." The foundational elements of any structure are proven by pressure. The same is true of our spiritual structures. The validity of God's principles are proven by stress. It is one thing to say, "The Bible says so" and it is something else to be able to add, "and I have proven this to be true in my own life."

When the tests come, we want to hear, "well done, thou good and faithful servant. Thou hast been faithful over a few things. I will make thee ruler over many." As you prove faithful in a few things (not small things, but few), God will add to your scope of influence and responsibility.

God has given us a general prescription for success in life. We have examined many promises of God, to be applied to different areas of our lives, but He has also given us a general overall formula in Psalm 1:1-2:

> Blessed is the man that walketh not in the counsel
> of the ungodly, nor standeth in the way of sinners,
> nor sitteth in the seat of the scornful. But his
> delight is in the law of the Lord; and in his law doth
> he meditate day and night.

This, in a nutshell, is God's prescription for successful living, for abundant life. Let's examine more closely the four crucial components or requirements we must meet in order to be blessed.

First, we are not to walk in the counsel of the ungodly. This means that we are not to act upon the advice of the individual who does not know the ways of God. The Scriptures indicate that we are not to accept the advice of the unregenerate man, whose counsel will always be from the natural man. Most of us would not seek advice from an out-and-out atheist, but we don't realize that the advice of the carnal Christian is just as dangerous. If a course of action is not clear to us after searching the Scriptures, we should seek out a mature Christian whose life is a testimony of his walk with God.

The second component is that we are not to stand in the way of sinners. The way of sinners is the path they take in life. We should remove ourselves from their paths—the broad and easy way to destruction. Solomon admonished, "My son, walk not thou in the way with them; refrain thy foot from their path" (Prov. 1:15). We are not to be like the sinners, or live the way sinners live. We must be with sinners at times, but God tells us not to participate in their ways with them. It is so very easy to adopt the manners and life style of the people you associate with, but the Bible warns us to keep ourselves from every evil, however small a transgression may seem. Paul wrote, "Abstain from every appearance of evil." Not only are we to abstain from evil, but also from situations which might be interpreted by others as being wrong. Our way should be clearly delineated from the "way of sinners."

The third element is that we are not to sit in the seat of the scornful. We all have had experiences with the scornful and know that few attitudes are as deadly and miserable as scorn. Notice that the scornful are depicted as sitting down. The scornful aren't doing anything; they are just sitting back criticizing and scoffing. Scorn can become a way of life, an attitude which permeates and dominates the life of a person who is a cynic. Both their words and attitudes minister death to everyone around them. All we have to do to become a scorner (it is very easy) is to pull up a chair and start condemning. Remember James' comment that "bless we God and curse we men, who are made after the similitude of God?" The scorner observes everything and everyone, the handiwork of God, with a critical eye. Because they are sitting, they are restricted. You can't do much if you're sitting. You can't even meet your own needs, much less the needs of others. In contrast, the Christian is running the good race, looking and hoping for the best in all.

While the first three components describe areas of personal restraint, the fourth one describes a positive action we must take. The first three were "don'ts." This one is a "do." "His delight is in the law of the Lord, and in his law doth he meditate day and night."

Let's discuss the law for a moment, because many Christians are confused about this subject. In this great renewal of the church, we tend to react adversely to those who stress keeping the law of God. To many, the mention of the law brings forth mental images of Moses with the stone tablets, endless sacrifices and ceremonies and, of course, the Pharisees. We read in the New Testament that the letter killeth, but the Spirit giveth life. Yet throughout the Old Testament, we find clear injunctions to keep God's laws. David wrote, "in the keeping of the law, there is great reward." God did not negate the Old Testament—it is still His Word. We no longer worship God according to the old covenant sealed with the blood of bulls and goats, but the books of the Old Testament are still the Word of God. Paul wrote that all Scripture is given to us for instruction, and was referring solely to the Old Testament, the only Scriptures he had. What is the solution, in light of Jesus' condemnation of legalism and attention to every jot and tittle of the law by the Pharisees?

To understand the law and its inherent purpose, we must first understand the very essence of God himself. "For God so loved the world that He gave. . . ." We know that God is love, but we must understand that the central theme of God's love is giving—the Creator gave of himself to His created. If we are to be the sons of God and take on the image of God, then our love must be a self-giving love to others.

Proving the Foundation

This is why Jesus, when questioned about the greatest commandment in the law, replied, "Thou shalt love the Lord thy God with all thy heart and with all thy soul and with all thy mind. This is the first and great commandment. And the second is like unto it. Thou shalt love thy neighbor as thyself." Notice carefully the final remark. "On these two commandments hang all the law and the prophets."

Jesus was saying that the central theme of all the law and everything that the prophets said was to promote self-giving love to God and man. The law and the purposes of the law need to be examined in the light of Jesus' statement. The law obviously places restraints upon man's actions. That much we already understand. But what actions does the law restrain? Self-serving ones. God has given us the law so that we can see that our actions—our natural and basic motivations—are self-serving. The law is a mirror to show us what we are like, and this is why the vast body of the law is negative. Thus, the law becomes, as Paul puts it, a schoolmaster to lead us to Christ.

When an individual carries out self-centered, self-serving actions, he sets up a chain of events which hurt not only himself but others as well. "Whatsoever a man soweth, that shall he also reap." A little playing around on the part of a husband results in a broken home and fatherless children; a little "keeping up with the Joneses" brings mounting bills and ulcers; a little "loan" from the company to tide you over brings conviction of embezzlement, shame and disgrace. Knowing and having set in motion the universal law of sowing and reaping, God says very simply, "Thou shalt not commit adultery; Thou shalt not covet; Thou shalt not steal." God, in His abundant love, has attempted to warn us, through the law, of the consequences of our destructive self-serving actions. We must come to realize that the law is actually God's safe harbor against the storms of ourselves.

Therefore, when we delight in and meditate upon God's law, as David wrote, we are building a fortress which will stand against the storms of life. When we study God's laws, we are studying God's non-optional principles of life. Living according to those principles will cause us to reap good fruit, not an unwanted crop of thorns.

What is the result of following God's formula for success? What will happen if we refrain from standing in the way of sinners, walking in the counsel of the ungodly, and sitting in the seat of scorners, and then make God's law our delight? The next verse tells us: "He shall be like a tree planted by the rivers of water, that bringeth forth his fruit in his season his leaf also shall not wither; and whatsoever he doeth shall prosper." The person who follows this formula will be like a tree planted by a river. What is a tree planted by a river like? It grows large and is deeply rooted. It is greener and more lush than inland trees. It bears fruit. Why? Because of its constant supply of water. The Psalmist was saying that we will prosper, become rooted deeply in God, and be fruitful, because we have a constant source of nourishment from the Spirit of God. Notice that the tree brings forth fruit in due season. You cannot make butter beans grow in January. You can't harvest wheat in April. God has ordained a season of planting and a season of harvesting, a time for all things under the sun. God has a season and a time appointed in our lives to produce fruit.

Notice also that the Psalmist wrote, "His leaf shall not wither, and whatsoever he doeth shall prosper." Joshua 1:8 reads: "This book of the law shall not depart out of thy mouth, but thou shalt meditate therein day and night, that thou mayest observe to do all that is written therein: for*then* shalt thou make thy way prosperous and then thou shalt have good success." If we fulfill the requirement, set forth by Joshua and repeated by the Psalmist, to meditate upon and delight in God's law, we cannot fail. When you come to a point in God that you love Him and meditate on His way and delight in Him, you cannot fail, because your will has been molded by His will—and His will cannot fail.

How do we reach that point? Can we just pray, "Lord, I delight in you. I meditate on your law. Therefore, make me like a tree planted by the rivers . . ." and expect it to be done immediately? No. It is a process that the Bible calls becoming established.

The Establishment

Becoming established in God doesn't mean being planted like a flower in one stationary place, but being planted in life so that you are not swayed or moved by circumstances, the economy of the nation, a fuel crisis, a rude neighbor, presidential elections, the threat of war, or an unpleasant work situation.

The first step in understanding the process of becoming established in God is to consider where you were when God found you. David gives this testimony, telling us where he was, and in a very real sense, where we all were before we knew God: "He brought me up also out of an horrible pit, out of the miry clay and set my feet upon a rock and established my goings" (Ps. 40:2).

Upon what rock did God place David's feet? Jesus. The Bible refers repeatedly to Jesus as the rock of our salvation. God rescues us from the horrible pit and miry clay of circumstances and lives without meaning. He picks us up out of the pit and sets us down on the firm foundation.

But after being rescued from the horrible pit, we must have our goings established. Second Thessalonians 2:16-17 reads: "Now our Lord Jesus Christ . . . comfort your hearts and establish you in every good word and work." The phrase "every good word and work," can be reduced to one word—actions, or what David calls our goings. Salvation then, the initial contact and belief in God, is not the end-all and be-all of God's plans for His children. He wants to establish our actions, and He does this by molding our attitudes.

God is always seeking to correct the attitudes of our hearts, whether we have been Christians for one year or fifty years. I am sure that some of God's most hard-hearted children are those who have been saved for years and years and they don't know that God is still seeking to perfect the attitudes of their hearts, an ongoing process. If your attitudes about life, people, and God have not undergone drastic changes since you met the Lord, I doubt that you ever met Him in the regeneration experience. You cannot come into a relationship with Jesus and remain the same, keeping the same attitudes you had before, because there was nothing godly at all about your attitudes before. Your attitudes may have been religious, but they weren't godly.

God's first step in establishing our goings is giving to us revelation about a certain attitude we have. He may say, "Son, there's something I want to discuss with you. I want to bring to your attention an attitude of self-righteousness in your heart. It's a wrong one, you know." You may say, "But look at what they said about me! I have a right to feel this way!" And you can go on for six months, six years, or sixty years and never become established in God.

Some people may raise the question, "Why is becoming established so important? The most important thing in the world is coming into a relationship with Christ—so what's all this other business about being established?" Remember the tree planted by the waters? That's the reason for becoming established. If a Christian never becomes established, he shall be like the tree planted in the desert that cannot produce fruit; his leaf shall wither, and whatsoever he does shall dry up and fail. That is not a Scripture, of course, but is an exact reversal of how David described the man who is established in God. It is not for God's sake that we become established, and go on to know the Lord, but for our sakes, our own happiness.

We've all met Christians who were indistinguishable in their lives and actions from non-Christians. And they are so miserable. They talk about being saved for twenty-three years, can tell you the exact date (which is good), but they live in painful turmoil, hurt, bitterness, and deep resentment from a wrong attitude that they have had for every single day of those twenty-three years and that God was not allowed to change. They may have their high spots during a particularly good sermon one Sunday, but generally their lives are as dark as the unbeliever's. They never allowed God to establish them. He brought them up out of the horrible pit and the miry clay, and set them on a rock, but He was never given permission to clean the muck off and establish their goings. So they never changed.

Often, Christians who really want to become established still refuse to let God show them their wrong attitudes—for a time. If we refuse to hear God's voice, we suffer continual pain brought on us by violation of God's spiritual laws. Refusal to hear God is followed by pain. It is not that God says, "Okay, since you refuse to hear, I'm going to send pain upon you." No. The law of gravity says that if you step off a roof, you will fall to the ground. A law of physics says if you exert enough pressure on a bone, it will break. So chances are, if you step off the roof, you will break something in your body. God doesn't say, "Well, Joe is about to step off the roof. I think I'll make him fall off and break a bone." No, the laws of the universe are in effect and everyone respects them. God's spiritual laws work with as much surety as God's natural laws.

You can choose to be pliable. You can say, "Lord, what is it? Show me my wrong attitude and show me how to correct it." As He reveals to you what the trouble is, you can say, "I see it, Lord. Please forgive me. Now, by your power, I ask you to change my heart. Show me the proper attitude. Take my wrong attitude and replace it with your attitude." Only by this process can we become established. Any person who has ever become a successful Christian has gone through this process. Every time a person repents and asks God to change his heart, he is following the process. Ask any successful Christian you know, and he will tell you how he has allowed God to change his heart. This process works and as you open yourself to God, not once, but as many times as He shines His light into the inner recesses of your soul, you will become more and more established.

Isaiah 7:9 reads: "If ye will not believe, surely ye shall not be established." After God has made the first move toward you, by bringing you up out of the horrible pit, you must say, "Lord God, I trust you with my life. You do with it what you will. You make the decisions and you direct the boat. I trust you. I believe you." If you do not believe or have enough confidence in God to give Him permission to direct your life, then you cannot be established. On the other hand, if you believe that God cares enough for you to guide and order every attitude, every thought, then you are already in the process of being established on the firm foundation.

Becoming New

It is very important that we fully understand—as much as we can with our limited minds—the magnitude of the miracle of rebirth, to see ourselves as God sees us and to know the depth of the horrible pit. To be saved means to be rescued from danger—imminent and immediate danger; it is a matter of urgency. To be redeemed means to be bought back—purchased—from the world, as one redeems something of value from a pawn shop. If you ever begin to feel unimportant and worthless in the sight of God, remind yourself that you are of great value to Him, so loved by Him that He paid the supreme price to buy you back from the world.

As we have said, there is more to God's work of saving us than bringing us up out of the horrible pit. The Scriptures tell us to to "be renewed in the spirit of your mind." We must be renewed, that is, made new again. After salvation comes the repair work. We must have an overhaul. Paul wrote: "If any man be in Christ, he is a new creature: old things are passed away; behold, all things are become new [or are in the process of becoming new or being made new]" (2 Cor. 5:17). This work is accomplished on the inner man. The damage done to us by the ways of the world has to be repaired and it is a slow, gradual process.

God doesn't fix us up with patches and splints, but with His own new parts, replacing areas of our lives and natures with His own life and nature. If you buy an old wrecked car and over the course of years, piece-by-piece and bolt-by-bolt you replace every part of the engine and the body with new parts, what do you have when you finish? Well, in one respect, you have the same old car. You still have an old 1962 Chevy with your doors. But in another sense, in all actuality, you have a brand new car.

How does God do this repair work? The Word is the changing power of God. The Word, remember, is the only agent we have for the cleansing of our attitudes, while the blood of Christ is the only agent we have for forgiveness. The Word renews the spirit of the mind. The Word replaces our attitudes with God's. Every Scripture, all that God has put forth in His Word, is designed to conform us to His likeness, to impart His character to us. The single largest cause of fatalities among Christians is neglect of the Word of God. As we run the race, we see the wrecked Christians by the side of the road. We can pray "Show me, Lord, Show me your attitudes," but unless you go to His Word, in which He has already revealed to us His attitudes, your prayer will be fruitless. The Word shows us the mind of Christ. The Bible has been called "The Manufacturer's Handbook" and neglecting the Word of God is a very dangerous thing for a Christian to do.

When you become established, you become settled and permanently founded upon the rock. In the parable of the house built upon the rock, Jesus said the winds came and beat against it, but it stood. When we are established upon the rock of our salvation, firmly entrenched in God, we will stand when the winds beat against us. We can be so firmly rooted in Christ that the only way we can move is if the rock moves—and that will never happen.

All the ways in which God speaks of our attachment to Him are in terms of security—anchored, established, planted, rooted, grounded; He is the shepherd, the captain of our salvation, the prince, mighty God, everlasting Father. We could get the impression that maybe God wants us to trust Him and be secure in the knowledge of Him! On the other hand, the hopes and promises of the world are spoken of in terms of insecurity in the Bible—the miry clay, sand, and webs. God has said that He is going to shake everything that can be shaken. The world is going to go berserk, but Christians, the peculiar people, will stand.

We cannot establish ourselves. We cannot become established by saying, "I'm going to hang on to the rock even if it kills me." It will kill you. You will fall and be hurt and disappointed. You will feel that God has let you down. What happened was that you did not allow God to do His work. If your establishment comes by your own efforts, you will fail when the winds come. If you allow God to establish you, earthquakes will happen all around you and you will never budge. "Except the Lord build the house, they labor in vain who build it" (Ps. 127:1).

First Peter 1:3-5 reads: "Blessed be the God and Father of our Lord Jesus Christ, which according to his abundant mercy hath begotten us again unto a lively hope by the resurrection of Jesus Christ from the dead, To an inheritance incorruptible, and undefiled, and that fadeth not away, reserved in heaven for you, Who are kept by the power of God through faith unto salvation ready to be revealed in the last time."

God is able both to build and to keep. Never has He failed to keep a child of His, and never has He discarded one. When Jesus was preparing to face the cross, He said, "Father, I have not lost any that you have given to me, except Judas, the son of perdition." Those who want, in their hearts, to stay with Christ will never be lost. It wasn't the strength of Peter that made him the dynamic Christian he became—he denied Christ three times. It wasn't the human efforts of Matthew, Luke, John, Paul, and Peter and all the others that enabled them to run the race. It was the changing power and the keeping power of God that had established these men.

Consider what effect the lives of these men had on all humanity. Think of the millions of people through the ages who drew strength from the lives and works of these early Christians, not to mention the numbers of people who come to the saving knowledge of Christ through the Gospels and Epistles those Christians wrote. These men—fishermen, tax collectors and tentmakers—laymen, allowed God to establish their lives in Him and direct their goings. And they turned the world upside down.

We often hear the comment in Christian circles today, "If

we only had a Peter or Paul to lead us." But you do—he's sitting right there on your pew! He's you. Just as God took the laymen of Jesus' day and established them in Him and sent them forth to change the world, He wants to establish you and send you forth.

You may say, "Who, me? I couldn't do anything like that." If so, you fall into the category of people to whom Jesus spoke, "Ye do err because ye know neither the scriptures nor the power of God." Let us not err and fall short of attaining God's purpose for our lives. Let us allow God's power to cause that Word to come to life in us and to enable us to be overcomers. This is being established in Him.

CHAPTER TWELVE

God's Secret Weapon

We have looked at God's principles concerning employment. We saw, too, that we must put these principles to work in our lives in order to be established. Now we need to discover why God wants us to be established.

The answer, the whole purpose of His extensive work in us, is found in these words: "Let your light so shine before men, that they may see your good works, and glorify your Father which is in heaven" (Matt. 5:16). This is the whole purpose for the overhaul God wants to accomplish in each life that is given to Him. He wants to bless us, and His work will result in rewards both material and spiritual for us individually, but then the end goal is others. First we learn God's principles; then, through testing and personal application, we become established; and then, we shine before men so that they can see our good works and glorify our Father. This is a continual pattern in maturing in God. First the learning, then the testing, and then the shining.

We all know that the hardest place to shine is at work, amidst the frustrations and unbelief. We find it a lot easier to shine on the gas station attendant, the waitress, and the door-to-door salesman, because we realize that these people do not know us or our shortcomings. The guys at work are the ones who see us every day and know us at our best—and worst. And when we try to witness to them, we can count on the fact that they will remember the worst a lot more than the best. We are the most vulnerable at work, because there is where we feel the least spiritual. All these factors combine to make witnessing to old Joe at work the hardest challenge of our Christian walk.

When we reach the point where we really desire God to use us at work, we invariably run into problems—with people, with relationships. We may have an intense desire in our hearts to introduce others to Jesus, but they don't seem interested in being introduced. Without a doubt, God will create circumstances which will give us opportunities to witness. But, if we are honest with ourselves, we have to admit that sometimes our witnessing doesn't seem effective, and we wonder what's wrong.

Imagine that Joe comes to work one morning with a severe hangover. He went to a big party the night before and today he is holding his head and looking for some Alka-Seltzer. He is in a rough state.

During the morning coffee break, Joe starts in telling everyone about his weekend. It was just great, he says. He did this, that and the other, but the grand finale was the party at Charles's. He had the best time he has ever had, he declares. He drank until three-thirty in the morning. He makes some remarks that make everyone laugh, except you. He tells how they had to carry Jim and some others out and put them in the car, since they could hardly stand up.

You are listening to all this and inside, you have a longing to tell Joe that there's a better way. You want to tell him, "Joe, don't you know that that's not life? That's not where it's at. That kind of life has no meaning." So you begin to pray, "Lord, give me an opportunity to share with poor Joe. He needs you so badly." Then, in a few minutes, you happen to meet Joe at the water cooler, where he is getting water to take some more Alka-Seltzer. Naturally, you think to yourself, "Aha! This is it! This is my chance."

You take a deep breath and start in. "Joe, I just happened to hear the things you were saying about everything you did at the party last night. I just want to tell you that Jesus loves you and wants to deliver you and set you free from all that emptiness." And you proceed to give him a capsule version of your testimony.

Joe just looks at you. Finally, after listening to you awhile, he says, "Now, look, just hold it a minute. Let me ask you a question. I have been listening to all this religious stuff now for two or three months. Every time we meet, you're always quoting Bible verses. I want to ask you something. What does Christianity offer that is better than what I have?"

You are aware that this is a significant question. You want to be sure to give him the right answer, so you silently pray before you answer.

"Joe, we have the greatest preacher you have ever heard in your life, and we get together on Wednesday nights at prayer meetings and it's just fantastic—we sing songs and the fellowship is so good and you can really sense the presence of God and . . . ." You go on trying to explain to him what you have, but it seems to be falling flat on the floor. You can tell he's not with you at all.

Finally, he interrupts. "I have heard all I want to hear. You tell me that you go to church, go to prayer meetings, and read the Bible—and you tell me it's fun. Well, the only thing I've ever seen is a bunch of long faces—I don't see all this peace and joy you talk about. And furthermore, I can't really believe that it's actually more fun to go to a prayer meeting than to a party. I had a ball last night. You tell me I didn't; but I know I did. Sure, I have a hangover this morning. I feel lousy and half sick to my stomach, but I tell you it's worth it. And next weekend, I'm going to party again—and the next weekend and the next."

You watch Joe recede into his office and you shake your head at the depth of Joe's darkness. You aren't reaching him. Why can't he see how empty his life is? Why can't he see how badly he needs God?

Levels of Life

In your encounter with Joe, the problem is the level of relationship on which you are seeking to operate in his life.

According to Bill Gothard, there are four different levels of relationships in life—acquaintances, casual friends, close friends, and intimate friends. An acquaintanceship is based on spasmodic personal contact. You simply know who someone is and you speak if you happen to run into him on the elevator. Much more contact than that develops a casual relationship. A casual relationship is based on common interests and concerns. You and your casual friend would both like the Yankees to win the World Series. You and your casual friend like fishing and tennis, and you both would like to see the company stay sound financially. But the friendship ends at five o'clock and you and he do not seek out each other's company away from the office. It is at this level that most co-workers operate, and that most Christians associate with non-Christians and vice versa. Casual friends may socialize on weekends but not on a regular or predetermined basis.

A close relationship is based on mutual (common) life goals. You and he have a strong bond of friendship and love; you seek each other's company out for family outings; you help and support each other with encouragement and perhaps on occasion materially. You talk about world problems and to some degree personal problems together. You describe him as "one of my very best friends."

The highest level of relationship is the intimate relationship, which is based upon commitment to the development of each other's character. You are devoted to seeking what is best for that person and you are committed to improving his character and he yours. In operation, this level of relationship is much like the close relationship, except that a commitment is involved. You discuss your hidden fears and goals together, without any fear of betrayed confidences. An intimate friendship can develop over any period of time, over a period of years, or over a period of just a few weeks. It is trust and love that undergirds this level of relationship.

Let's go back to Joe at the water cooler. For your part, you are committed to the betterment of Joe. You are committed to improving Joe's character in a Christian sense, by introducing him to a better way of life. You are attempting to operate on the level of an intimate friend. Joe, on the other hand, is not the least bit interested in either you or the betterment of his character. He just wants you to leave him alone. He even likes himself the way he is and you can't convince him that he doesn't. Furthermore, he didn't ask you to comment on his character or way of life. He is happy the way he is, and you are an intruder. He considers you just another guy in the office—a little bit fanatic, but a nice guy, maybe.

Jesus had something like these levels of relationships in mind when He said, "Don't cast your pearls before swine." It's not that He considered these people pigs; it's that you should not take something so precious and beautiful to you as your experience with the Lord and throw it in front of someone who has no sensitivity for the beauty of that pearl. Pigs have extremely poor eyesight and like Joe simply cannot see. It's not that you hate pigs, either; it's just that to people in darkness, with such poor sight, your pearl is indistinguishable from all the other garbage that is thrown in front of them. That's what happened to you at the water fountain with Joe. You displayed your pearls, the things in your life that are precious to you, and due to his insensitivity and spiritual blindness, Joe brushed them aside and walked away.

Just as we operate on different levels of relationships with people in life, so we also operate on different levels spiritually also. We have grown to different heights on the spiritual ladder. This is why we speak of spiritual babes and spiritual giants and the process of maturing in Christ. You have been touched by the living God, filled with His Holy Spirit, and now have a vital, living relationship with Him. That puts you several rungs on the spiritual ladder above the bottom, where Joe lives. You are living in the light and as you look down you see Joe and others groping around in darkness. As you watch Joe, you have a desire and longing to see those at the bottom come up the ladder and share in the joys of the light with you. When you witness to Joe, you are saying essentially, "Hey, Joe, come on up here. It's great." But Joe, who is insensitive to light, says, "Why should I? I like it just fine down here."

What is the solution then? How can we accomplish our mission, the goals God has set before us if Joe won't even listen? How can he ever know God if he won't even give Christians a chance to explain the gospel to him? We need to aim to create a desire in Joe to ascend, to come up the steps into the light. We can't make Joe drink the living water, but we can make him awfully thirsty. That is God's solution.

Think back on your own life to the time before you met the Lord, if you came to Him as an adult. Were you the least bit interested in knowing Him at first? No, most likely, you weren't. Can you see a point in your life when you began to become interested? God began to draw you, until finally, the day came when you said, "Lord God, I want to know you." What did it? How did you get to that point? It was the Word of God, either written or verbal, or in some form. You had heard a sermon, or a neighbor witnessed, or you heard a testimony. That night, or a week, month, or year later, you came to the Lord. It takes the Word of God to create a desire to know God. The Word is a creative force, active and alive. The Word is the only force we have with which to stir a desire in people to know the living God.

Ezekiel 36:26 reads: "A new heart also will I give you, and a new spirit will I put within you: and I will take away the stony heart out of your flesh, and I will give you an heart of flesh." The unregenerate heart is as dead and hard as a rock. Nothing can be done to remold it, fix it, reform it, repair it, or make it soft. There is no recourse except for God to remove it entirely and replace it with a new and different heart. He calls it a heart of flesh.

Here is Joe, then, with his stony heart. He loves to party on weekends. He won't go to church. He won't read the Scriptures. He won't watch Oral Roberts or the 700 Club on television. Every time the Word of God comes to him, by gospel tracts or *Guideposts* magazine or a radio broadcast by Billy Graham, or from you at work, he throws up a block. He immediately identifies these messages as religious and he doesn't want anything to do with it. He throws the written material in the garbage can and simply tunes out the verbal messages. How, then, are you to get through to him? How can you reach a man who refuses to avail himself of the Word of God, the only force which can reach him?

You have already gone to Joe and tried to share the gospel with him. But far from creating a desire in him to know God, you succeeded only in creating a desire in him to get away from you as quickly as possible.

The solution to the dilemma lies in the fact that the Bible is not the only edition of the Word of God. According to the Scriptures, God has "published" the Word in seven editions.* The first is written on nature (Ps. 19:1). The second is the Word written on the conscience of men (Rom. 2:15). The third edition is written on tables of stone (Exod. 24:12). The fourth edition is the written Word, the Scriptures (Rom. 15:4). The fifth edition is the Word made flesh, Jesus, the illustrated edition (John 1:14). The sixth edition is the believer, with the Word written on his heart (Heb. 8:10). The seventh and last edition is the outward Christian life, called the living epistle (2 Cor. 3:2-3).

The seventh edition holds the key for us in discovering how we can witness to Joe. This edition is God's secret weapon, intended for use at the close of the age. The time is now and the weapon is you. Paul wrote:

> Ye are our epistle written in our hearts, known and read of all men: forasmuch as ye are manifestly declared to be the epistle of Christ ministered by us, written not with ink, but with the Spirit of the living God; not in tables of stone, but in fleshy tables of the heart.

You must be the living Word at work. As we saw in Chapter one, Christians and non-Christians naturally tend to segregate. You won't join in with Joe in worldly activities and Joe won't join in with you in spiritual activities. God then has designed work as the common denominator for the Christian and non-Christian, and the office as that place where the Christian must meet the non-Christian world. For the very reason that the office is the hardest place to shine, you must shine there as the living Word, known and

---

* Frank Charles Thompson, *The New Chain Reference Bible* (B.B. Kirkbride Bible Co., 1974).

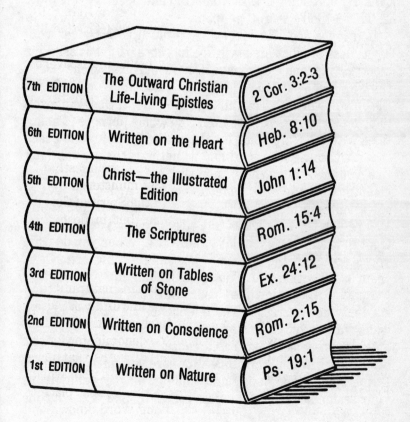

read by all men.

SEVEN EDITIONS OF THE WORD OF GOD

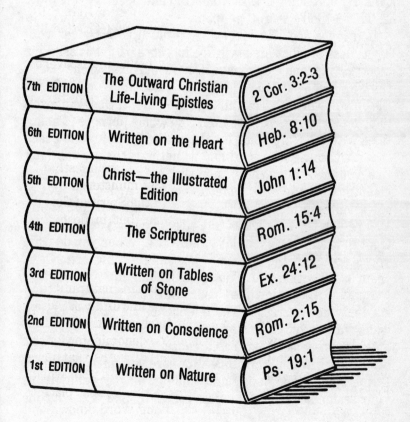

7th EDITION	The Outward Christian Life-Living Epistles	2 Cor. 3:2-3
6th EDITION	Written on the Heart	Heb. 8:10
5th EDITION	Christ—the Illustrated Edition	John 1:14
4th EDITION	The Scriptures	Rom. 15:4
3rd EDITION	Written on Tables of Stone	Ex. 24:12
2nd EDITION	Written on Conscience	Rom. 2:15
1st EDITION	Written on Nature	Ps. 19:1

THE CHRISTIAN EMPLOYEE

Joe has no desire to sit down with you and discuss the truth and value of Jesus' words: "Love your enemies, bless them that curse you, do good to them that hate you, and pray for them which despitefully use you, and persecute you" (Matt. 5:44). But whenever he sees you do these things before his very eyes at work, he is actually reading Matthew 5:44. He is reading the Word of God and doesn't even know it. This is God's secret weapon.

God loves Joe. He loves Joe as much as He loves you, regardless of what life style Joe has chosen. Jesus shed his blood for Joe, and would have if there had been no one else in the world who needed redemption. Since the Word of God is the only power which can change Joe's heart, God wants you to bring forth the Word to him. The whole purpose of being filled with the Holy Spirit is to be so filled with joy and peace that it will cause others to know something, to see something that you have, something good that they want. Before you attempt to witness to someone verbally about the joys of salvation, you must live the joy of salvation before them. Before you try to witness to God's love and peace, live, in front of their very eyes, love and peace. When you do this, you can count on the fact that something is going on inside of them as they read you. The seed is falling into their lives.

Imagine a situation like this: at work one day, everything suddenly goes berserk. The telephones are ringing off the walls with angry callers or harsh orders. Everyone is mad at everyone else. There is a tension you can feel in the atmosphere around the office. But here you come. You walk through the office happy and smiling, quietly going about your assigned duties. The boss comes by and takes out his frustration and anger on you.

"When is that structural design for Thomas Company going to be ready?" the boss asks you impatiently. "It was supposed to be finished yesterday afternoon, and if we lose this client, Tom, there are going to be some surprises around here. . . ."

"Sir," you begin calmly. "Everything is ready for the final computer run, but the repairmen still don't have the computer fixed. I just called the computer department and I was told the computer should be functioning by three o'clock this afternoon. . . ."

"Three o'clock! Listen here, Tom, you better have that design first thing in the morning. I don't care if they have it fixed at three or seven—you just better have it at eight in the morning sharp. If you or anybody in this company ever did everything right I sure don't remember when. . . ."

"Sir, I'll have the design ready for you even if I have to stay here until midnight," you agree peaceably.

"Just be sure that you do," the boss snaps.

"Yes, sir," you reply as he turns on his heels and walks away, grumbling about his worthless employees.

Old Joe is sitting there nursing his hangover, just trying to get through the day in one piece. He is watching you. "Oh, I just don't believe that guy," he thinks. You walk by again and again. Joe sees that you are exhibiting joy and peace and contentment in the midst of this crisis. He can't figure it out. The seed of the Word is beginning to irritate him a little.

Just as he is dropping his fourth Alka-Seltzer of the day in his glass, you walk by for the twenty-fifth time, smiling a lot and humming a little tune. He just stares at you, wondering. What has really happened is that Joe has read almost the whole book of Ephesians, or several Psalms. The Word has come forth to him. Your light, the light that Jesus, the living Word, has created in your life, is shining on Joe, shining in his darkness. He has read about patience, peace, forgiveness, obedience, hope and love. He has read the Word of God. It came to him in a form that he couldn't throw in the garbage can or tune out. And it came to him in a form that he couldn't dismiss with a shrug. Paul wrote, "Against these things [the fruits of the Holy Spirit], there is no law." Joe can't do anything against them. He has read the Word of God in a form that he couldn't turn his back on.

When someone reads the Word of God, something is going to happen. "So shall my word be that goeth forth out of my mouth: it shall not return unto me void, but it shall accomplish that which I please, and it shall prosper in the thing whereto I sent it" (Isa. 55:11). Joe has read the Word of God and something will be accomplished in him. God will create something in him—the desire to ascend.

The Word has a living, creative power. It is a two-edged sword that separates bone from marrow. It performs surgery of the heart. It has power. It was with the Word that God created the universe; it is with the Word that He breaks the stony heart into pieces.

At this point, however, Joe doesn't particularly want to be a Christian. He still doesn't want to give up his weekend partying, which is the first thing that comes to his mind when he thinks of God. He doesn't really want to know God; he just wants peace. He wants to get rid of his acid indigestion. His motives are purely selfish, but a selfishness motivates many people who come to the Lord. I didn't want to become a Christian at first. I did not want to become and do those things I associated with Christianity. My sole motive was that I did not want to go to hell. It was fear that prompted me to seek God at first. So Joe doesn't want to be a Christian; but he does want something that you have. He is beginning to want to ascend to where you are.

You have walked through the office in front of Joe throughout the day. He has seen the whole army of God parade before his eyes. He has seen David singing praises to God. He has read about Paul and Silas in prison, praising

God at midnight, in the depths of a crisis. He has read that Jesus forgave His persecutors as He hung on the cross. About the thirtieth time you walk by, Joe can't stand it any more. He is just about to pop.

"Hey, fella," he calls you over. "Let me ask you a question. In all this turmoil here at the office, how can you be so happy? This is the worst day we've ever had. Aren't you even human—how could you listen to the boss talk to you that way and not get mad? Don't you know that he has threatened to fire all of us if we can't meet our quota this month?"

Look at this. Joe has asked you a question. He has approached you. He has seen something of benefit in your life style and he is asking you how you live like you do. He has flung open the door of opportunity and demanded that you come in. He knows full well that the boss treated you unjustly; he knows you had no control over the situation which caused the delay; he knows full well that you know you weren't responsible—so how can you act this way?

First Peter 3:15 reads: "But sanctify the Lord God in your hearts: and be ready always to give an answer to every man that asketh you a reason of the hope that is in you." Be ready to answer Joe. The way we sanctify the Lord God in our hearts is by living the Word, living Jesus. Your hope will show; others will notice it, for you are known and read. Paul knew that when you live the Word, people are going to ask you questions. They are going to ask you "how can you?. . ." Anticipate it and be ready. Be sensitive and have your radar tuned for it. Often we don't even recognize that important question. Some may say, "Hey, you're grinning like a Cheshire cat—what are you so cheerful about?" When the question comes, you have been invited into that person's life, into his realm of thinking.

Now, you try to answer Joe. "You know, situations like

this used to tear me up. But I met a man who said he'd give me peace." Joe quickly says, "Who? What are you talking about?" And you answer, "Jesus. He said 'My peace I give you, not as the world gives peace, but as God gives peace.' He really does it too!"

Now, Joe may give you his disgusted look, and roll his eyes and say, "Oh, I see," and abruptly end the conversation. Inside he's thinking, "More religious stuff. I should have known."

Was the whole thing a failure just because Joe didn't like the answer to his question? No. The important part is that Joe had asked the question. That is all that matters. Let's see why questions are so important.

Jesus said this about questions: "And I say unto you, Ask, and it shall be given you; seek, and ye shall find; knock, and it shall be opened unto you. For every one that asketh, receiveth; and he that seeketh findeth; and to him that knocketh it shall be opened (Luke 11:9). Joe has asked. He has sought. He has knocked. What does Jesus say will happen? Joe will get his answer. Jesus didn't say Joe might get his answer, but that he would. It is definite.

Now Joe doesn't know this promise of God. But does his ignorance about God change or affect God or the validity of God's Word? No; no more than unbelief changes the truth of the gospel. The Word of God is just as powerful whether Joe believes it and accepts it or not. And when Joe asks and receives, a powerful seed is planted.

Jesus used this principle of witnessing in proclaiming the gospel. We tend to think of Jesus as a man who overwhelmed people with His power, so that everyone knew He was the Son of God. But if we examine the Bible, we find that Jesus often created hunger—or sometimes just curiosity—everywhere He went, often prompting the question, "What manner of man is this? . . ." The people did not know who He was. Isn't this what Joe was seeking when he asked, "What kind of man are you? . . ."

A good example of Jesus—and Joe—is found in John 4. Jesus was traveling to Samaria, and sent His disciples on ahead to buy some lunch. As he entered the city, he stopped at Jacob's well. There, a woman, a Samaritan was drawing water.

Jesus walks up to her and asks for a drink of water. He didn't say, "Woman, I am the Lamb of God. Believe on me and be saved. I am the promised Messiah of Israel." Most likely, she would have understood these statements, but He wanted to create a desire in her to know first. There was nothing spiritual about His words at all. He just wanted a drink of water.

She replies, "How is it that thou being a Jew, asketh drink of me, which am a woman of Samaria? for the Jews have no dealings with the Samaritans."

Ah! She saw something in His act of asking for water. It was unusual, out of character for a Jew. Like Joe, after seeing you remain calm and even happy in the face of ranting, angry and unjust boss, the woman had to know, "How is it that you can? . . ." She did not know that she was reading the Word made flesh, reading that "God is no respecter of persons."

Jesus tells her: "If thou knewest the gift of God, and who it is that saith to thee, Give me to drink; thou wouldest have asked of him and he would have given thee living water."

Jesus ignores her question about a Jew associating with a Samaritan. He says, "If you only knew who I am, you would ask me for water." He really has her curiosity up now. He has whetted her appetite and her desire to know is growing. He is aiming, maneuvering His words, to get her permission to step into her life.

The woman says: "Sir, thou hast nothing to draw with,

and the well is deep: from whence hast thou that living water? Art thou greater than our father Jacob, which gave us the well, and drank thereof himself and his children and his cattle?"

She is saying, "Why, you don't even have a bucket. You aren't greater than Jacob, who dug the well in the first place. Where do you think you are going to get water?"

Now, if Joe said to you, "Look, buddy, who do you think you are? My father was a good man, and he didn't have any religion. You Christians just think you're better than everyone else." You would probably want to back off right then, wouldn't you?

Jesus' answer to the woman is very important in creating her desire to ascend. "Whosoever drinketh of this water shall thirst again: but whosoever drinketh of the water that I shall give him shall never thirst; but the water that I shall give him shall be in him a well of water springing up into everlasting life."

Jesus has again ignored her specific question. He did not defend himself against the charge that He was no greater than Jacob. He didn't get into theology. He didn't talk about a bucket. He just continued to talk to her about the living water.

Look at the effect these words had on this woman. "Sir, give me this water."

Give me this water. She has asked Him for something. She didn't understand it fully. She didn't know that He was speaking of eternal life. But she asked Him for this wonderful water He said He had. She wanted it. She got it!

The purpose of becoming established in God is to so live that a desire, a thirst, is created in others. Jesus was so established in the Father that He could say, "I say nothing but what my Father speaks. I do nothing but what my Father does." Letting your light shine does not mean spouting religious words all the time. It means living a life flowing with the fruit of the Holy Spirit.

Proverbs 11:30 reads: "He that winneth souls is wise." Jesus was wise. He was displaying wisdom in His approach to the Samaritan woman. We can partake of that same wisdom. How? "If any of you lack wisdom, let him ask" (James 1:5). What happens if we ask? We receive. The whole ability, the whole power of God, is available to us if we but ask. And James tells us that we have not because we ask not.

A friend of mine proved the validity and success of living as the Word for others to read. My friend, Wayne, became a living epistle and one man in particular read Jesus, the Word of God, in his life.

Wayne had several different field crews working for him in his line of work, and the field crews had rough, dirty work, done in all kinds of terrain and in all kinds of weather. As a rule, the men on the crews had to be as rough as their work, and they were. There was one particular man on one of the crews who weighed about three hundred pounds and none of it was fat. He could and did consume vast quantities of alcohol without getting unruly, but over the years he had become a hard-core alcoholic. But then something began to happen.

This man had been watching and reading Wayne. Just as we imagined in the case of Joe, reading you thirty-two times in one day, this man was reading Wayne, a living epistle, and finally, his desire to know was overwhelming. Early one morning, Wayne was sitting at his desk, when all of a sudden, the door was thrown open, slammed against the wall, and this enormous man came barging in. He slammed the door behind him. He was obviously upset about something.

"Okay, what do you want from me," he yelled, leaning

over the desk right in Wayne's face. "What is it you want out of me? I know you have something up your sleeve and I want to know what it is!"

Wayne was a good size himself, but clearly no match for this man, who was upset enough to become violent. Finally Wayne was able to get him to sit down.

"I don't want anything from you," Wayne began. "Just explain to me what this is all about. What makes you think I want anything from you?"

"Well, I don't know what's going on around here," the man said with evident frustration. "But for the last two or three months, something's been going on. You are butterin' me up for something and I want to know what you're up to."

Wayne encouraged him to explain further, repeating that he didn't want anything from him.

"Well," the man said, "you used to not care whether I got up or went to bed, whether I lived or died. You didn't care about me in any way. And now, for two months, every time I see you, you're asking me how I'm doing, if I feel okay, how's my family, if everything's going okay. You're not doing this for nothing. Now, what is it you want from me?"

Look at what has happened. This man read the Word for two months. He read, "Care for each other affectionately with brotherly love." He read, "Love one another, even as I [Jesus] have loved you." For two months, he read all about God's love, and finally he exploded with a desire to know.

Wayne explained to him what had happened. He told him that Jesus had come into his life and that yes, he had changed. He was a different person now and had a love for people. He told him all about the gospel.

It really burned this guy up. He had asked the question, gotten the answer, but didn't like it. He left Wayne's office about an hour later. But he had heard the Word.

The Word began to get under his skin, heading for his

heart actually. He wrestled with it that whole week while he was on the road with the crew. The following Friday, he went home and told his wife what had happened and all that Wayne had said. The Word, from a living epistle, had gone forth. He picked up the telephone and invited Wayne to come over and tell him more about what had happened to him. Wayne went to his house and spent two or three hours with the man and his wife, simply explaining to them the plan of salvation.

Still, by the time Wayne left, the man did not want to accept Jesus. But then, when Wayne was gone, the man went to his bedside, knelt down and prayed, "Lord God, if you are there, and if all those things that fella told me are true, I want to know you. I give you my alcohol. I give you my life. I give you everything if you can do for me what you did for that guy." Jesus answered that prayer even as the words were spoken and the man had a tremendous experience with the Lord. He was instantly delivered from alcohol, and on the following Monday morning, he was telling everyone within hearing distance about Jesus.

Wayne never planned or rehearsed to witness to this man. It just happened. The living Word went forth and could not return unto God empty. The Word was planted in the man's life, creating in him a desire to know, and breaking the stony heart.

The Light

There is yet another important factor or truth to remember in witnessing to people. In Revelation 3:20, Jesus said, "Behold, I stand at the door and knock: if any man hear my voice, and open the door, I will come into him and will sup with him, and he with me."

Who is standing and knocking for admittance at Joe's door? Jesus is. When we witness to someone, we sometimes get the feeling that we are knocking on Joe's door, and sometimes we would like to knock it down. We must remember, however, that when we witness to Joe, it is Jesus knocking; the transaction is between Joe and Jesus, not Joe and you.

Picture this illustration. Joe lives in a house, with a front door. He has no electricity at all, and the whole house is pitch black. Joe lives in total darkness. Joe just sleeps all the time and has no joy or life in his house at all. For a long time Jesus has been standing outside the front door, gently knocking. At last, Joe feels a strange stirring, and he realizes that someone is knocking on his front door. He opens it and when he sees who's there, that this has something to do with religion or church or something along those lines, he slams the door shut. Joe's question is his act of opening the door. He sees something strange, and he asks you a question, "How is it? . . ." He has opened the door just slightly to see.

But even though Joe shuts the door angrily, something has still happened. In the Bible, Jesus is described as the light of men; people who do not know God are living in darkness. Think for a moment about the nature of light. The speed of light is unexcelled—and the presence of light destroys darkness. Light penetrates darkness, but darkness can never penetrate light, because light is a presence, but darkness is only the lack of light. So here is Joe's house, in total darkness, and Jesus, a brilliant light, is right outside the door. Now, what happened when Joe opened the door just slightly to see who was there? The light happened (John 1:9).

No matter how fast Joe shut the door, the light flooded into his living room. The light hit the walls and pictures and bounced and reflected throughout his house. How does Joe react? With anger and disgust. Why? Because the light is very painful to him. He slammed the door, but the light, Jesus, the Word, got into Joe's house. It will begin to bother him and act upon him.

One wonderful characteristic about Jesus is that He never leaves the door. Initial rejection does not make Him give up. He said, "I stand at the door and knock." That is, He stands and knocks continually. In Joel and in Acts, it is written that in the latter days God will pour out His Spirit upon all flesh. Not just on Christian flesh, but on all flesh. Jesus is always outside Joe's door, continually knocking.

When the door is opened just a crack, the light pours in. It is going to create a desire in that individual to know more. Joe begins to seek. And God will meet him and answer him.

At a point in my life, I began to ask questions, to open the door just slightly. I began to get hungry because the Word had come to me from living epistles. Life was empty to me and I wanted answers. I was asking questions inside, but every time I opened the door, the light hurt. It caused pain. It caused confusion. But the gnawing pressure created by the Word began to perform its work, creating a desire to know and breaking the stony heart. I had tasted and had seen the potential for something I wanted. But I didn't want to be a Christian, because of the image I had of Christianity. I tried to shut it out of my mind, but it kept coming back. Finally, I opened the door wide and said, "Come on in, Lord Jesus."

When the Word is made flesh in your life, and dwells at your place of work, questions will be asked—and answered.

CHAPTER THIRTEEN

The Wonderful World of Sight and Sound

We have seen that God desires to form us into "living epistles, known and read of all men." We know, then, what we are to become—living epistles, and why we are to become this—to be known and read of all men. We know also how to become living epistles—by allowing God to establish us upon the rock. We need to know now how we are "known and read of all men." How do other people read us? Others may know we are Christians by our own confessions, but how, actually and specifically, do they read us?

We become living epistles as God removes our natural attitudes and replaces them with the attitudes of Christ. But, if you will remember, attitudes are a condition of the heart, and cannot be discerned directly by others. People sense or detect our attitudes by our actions. The attitude is not in itself transmittable. It must be put into action, and it will be, whether we want it to or not. "As a man thinketh in his heart, so is he."

God has created the human being with five external senses—smell, taste, sight, hearing and touch. Of these five, two senses, sight and hearing, are used primarily to communicate our attitudes to others. By sight and sound we reveal our attitudes and thus the living Word to others. By sight and sound do others read us. As Joe plowed through his day, he transmitted by sharp words and the look on his face his inner attitudes. By Joe's criticism and frowns, his secretary read his inner man, which in that case was pretty dark. Let's examine first the importance of sight to determine how people read our looks.

When someone looks at us, he looks primarily at our faces, but sees more than just the physical features. He sees the expression, the mood, which is a reflector of attitudes. The Bible calls this total appearance the countenance. Depression, joy, sorrow, happiness, discouragement, encouragement, cheerfulness, or gloom can appear on our countenances.

Your countenance will show your personality, the inner man. If, then, you are a born-again Christian, your new inner man should show on your countenance—but does it? You may say, "Oh, but we can't help what we look like!" But you can. You cannot change your physical features, but you can change your physical expression, your countenance. Jesus said, "Let your light shine. . . ." Allow it to shine. You can have control of your light to let it shine or to conceal it. "Ye are the light of the world. A city that is set on an hill cannot be hid. Neither do men light a candle and put it under a bushel, but on a candlestick; and it giveth light unto all that are in the house. Let your light so shine before men, that they may see your good works and glorify your Father which is in heaven" (Matt. 5:14-16).

Permit your light to shine, so that others may see your good works (actions) and glorify God. Philippians 2:15 makes much the same statement from a slightly different perspective: "That ye may be blameless and harmless, the sons of God, without rebuke, in the midst of a crooked and perverse nation, among whom ye shine as lights in the world." No one would argue with the belief that the world today is "crooked and perverse." Our response? We are to shine.

How do we shine? We know that Jesus did not mean for us to radiate actual, physical light or He would have given us halos. What did He mean then by shine? We know that we have the light because we know God; but Jesus said that we should not only shine, but shine so that others could see it. How? The Word of God answers this question by comparing us to mirrors.

> But all of us who are Christians have no veils on our faces, but reflect like mirrors the glory of the Lord. We are transformed in ever-increasing splendor into His own image, and this is the work of the Lord who is the Spirit. (2 Cor. 3:18, Phillips)

The primary characteristic of a mirror is that it reflects whatever its surface sees. Our faces are mirrors; what appears in our faces is the countenance. We, as mirrors, are to look to Jesus. When we do, the glory of God is reflected in our countenances to those who look at us.

In this Scripture, notice that our faces are unveiled. If you cover a mirror with a veil, the only thing that will appear in the mirror is the back of the veil! The veil effectively prevents us from reflecting the glory of God. We obviously can, then, look toward Jesus, but with a veiled face. A veil can be any number of spiritual problems which are inevitably of our own doing. God never puts up a veil. When Jesus died on the cross, the veil in the holy of holies, representing the sacred presence of God himself was rent in two, destroying the veil which separated man from God forever. We, however, are proud. We refuse to submit, or to repent. We are stiff-necked. These are the attitudes with which we veil our faces. The veil could even be of loose-weave so that we can see Him to a degree, but the image will be distorted and hazy and partial. In turn, people will see a hazy and distorted and partial picture of the glory of God.

As we reflect the glory of God, we actually become what we reflect. The human mirror, unlike glass mirrors, is gradually transformed into what it reflects. We have all known elderly couples who have lived happily together for so many years that they have begun to look like each other. And we know that if we look at something long enough, as in coveting, we eventually do something about it, to procure it for ourselves. Exposure to any situation, indeed, will produce an indelibly etched memory. As you look at Jesus, you are actually being shaped and conformed to His likeness.

Psalm 34:5 reads: "They looked unto him and were lightened [radiant]." We are to radiate His glory. When we hear the word glory, we generally think of the cloud that moved in front of the children of Israel in the wilderness, or the shekina glory that came down and consumed the sacrifice on the altar; but here, we need to understand glory as meaning the character of God, the visible personality of Jesus.

Imagine that you are sitting at your desk one day, and Harry comes in, staggering under the load of several boxes. You watch him a minute, hoping that someone will offer to help him, but a quick glance tells you that you are the only one who sees Harry struggling with the heavy boxes. "I'm so busy right now," you say to yourself, "if I offer to help him, I'll end up helping him sort them too—but I know I ought to help." You know you are not that busy and that you are just being selfish. That makes you feel guilty, so you finally get up to help Harry. "I'm going to be a good Christian," you say to yourself.

"Let me help you, Harry," you volunteer with as much cheerfulness as you can muster. He thanks you wholeheartedly and together you and he carry the boxes up two flights of stairs to the storage room, and now you are stuck with sorting them, just as you expected. By that time you are feeling like a martyr and you accordingly put on a martyred expression, so that Harry will realize that your help was a big sacrifice. He sees a pious and gloomy look on your face—and now he feels guilty for putting you through this. A few more minutes of gloom pass, and Harry begins to feel angry. He thinks to himself, "Why is he looking so put upon. If he didn't want to help, he shouldn't have offered in the first place." All this time, you are acting like you are being so very helpful.

Did you have your eyes on Jesus? Of course not. The glory of God did not appear on your countenance. Darkness appeared on your countenance. You did not say one wrong word; it was all in your countenance.

Now let's examine the world of words. The Bible has a lot to say about the importance of words. One of the strongest statements God makes is in Proverbs 18:21: "Death and life are in the power of the tongue." In the story of Korah, we saw that death, the literal deaths of 14,953 Israelites, resulted because of Korah's words. He could have sulked in his heart all he wanted, but until the words were spoken, nothing would have resulted, except that he would have stewed in his juices to his own harm. His words did the damage. His tongue killed all those Israelites.

But the tongue also has the power of life. Our tongues can be instruments to impart life. Korah could have proven this. Moses did prove it on numerous occasions, when he interceded for the nation, speaking to God with life-giving words.

Isaiah 50:4 reads: "The Lord God hath given me the

tongue of the learned, that I should know how to speak a word in season to him that is weary." Do you want to learn to witness to others? Then learn to speak a word in season to him that is weary. God wants us to learn to speak in season, that is, at the proper time. As your wife is pulling burned toast out of the oven is not the time to tell her what a good cook she is. As Harry is recovering from a tongue-lashing from the boss is not the time to tell him he has been selected to present the boss a gift at the annual company banquet. As a friend is recovering from the death of a loved one is not the time to tell him his grief is a lack of faith.

If your secretary has typed a report five times because of errors, and is embarrassed and disgusted with herself, she qualifies to be counted among the weary. It is not the time to compliment her on her typing as she throws the twenty-eighth sheet of paper into the garbage can. If she hears you say, "Sue, you are a very good typist," at the same moment she pulls the twenty-ninth sheet out of her typewriter, she will take your words as sarcasm, no matter how good your intentions were. Your word was appropriate; your timing was not. It was not in season. If you had waited fifteen minutes, after the report was finished, then said, "Look, don't worry about that report. You worked hard and did a good job and I appreciate your effort. Don't be nervous about it." How much better it is to speak a word with the tongue of the learned in season.

Isaiah was not talking about religious words, spiritual-sounding words, but normal, everyday conversation. We need to learn to use, pick and control words of encouragement, with sensitivity toward those who are weary, hurt and discouraged. When we learn how to speak effectively to people, God can use us later, when the time comes for religious conversation.

We have all encountered tactless people. Tactlessness is really only a lack of sensitivity and a carelessness with words. It's not incurable; it can be overcome with determination to speak in season. If you are tactless, and your tactlessness hurts another person, then some later time when you try to witness to that person about God's love for him or her, the "victim" reacts, "Uh! A lot this guy knows about love!" It is very important that we learn to use words.

Proverbs 16:24 reads: "Pleasant words are as an honeycomb, sweet to the soul and health to the bones." A person may come by the office to visit Joe and find his secretary upset. If this person knows how to say a word with the tongue of the learned in season, he will sit down and just talk with her. He may not share anything of a spiritual nature with her at all; he may just comfort her, reassure her, and calm her, or maybe just get her to talk about it. He will speak a word of encouragement and his words will come to her like honey. They bring sweetness to her personality, her soul, and health to her body. Honey is very thick and viscous. It has a soothing quality because of its texture. We drink honey in tea for a sore and scratchy throat. In the case of a person, whose personality has been scratched by something, pleasant words, like honey, have a healing quality.

Health to the bones: that's an interesting phrase. Some doctors think ninety percent of our illnesses are psychosomatic in origin. They begin in a mental state and end up in the physical state. The illness really does exist; it is not imaginary, yet its cause and origin is in the mind. The classic example is an ulcer. You worry and are consumed in anxiety and before long, you have a hole in your stomach. That hole is very real; but it was really put there by the fears and worries of your mind. Pleasant words, which heal us of worry, depression, fear, and discouragement, can actually affect our health.

To those people we see daily, our colleagues at work, we need to learn to speak wisely, pleasantly and in season. We can produce with our words, a sweetness and health within an individual without their even being aware of what we are doing. They will not even be aware that the changes they are experiencing in their personalities have anything to do with God, Jesus, or Christianity. Yet these changes can be a softening, a preparation for the day when they come to the saving knowledge of Christ. We have become accustomed to believing that witnessing means only religious words, but this is far from the whole and sum of manifesting God to others.

"A wholesome tongue is a tree of life" (Prov. 15:4). When man fell from Paradise, he lost the privilege of eating from which tree? The tree of life. He lost access to the life-giving tree God had provided. Is it not significant then, that God compares a wholesome tongue with a tree of life? God has provided another tree of life for us and it's growing right inside our mouths. The book of James enumerates the dangers of the tongue, the most unruly member of the body. We need to choose who will be in control of our tongues—the flesh, or the Spirit? God wants each of us to come to the point that we will allow Him to control our tongues, make them wholesome, so they can be trees of life to others around us.

Not only must we use wise and wholesome words, but also use a wise and wholesome tone of voice. "A soft answer turneth away wrath" (Prov. 15:1). People hear the inflection and spirit of our words as well as the actual words. I know some children who play a rather interesting game with their household pet. You may try it with your dog—you will feel fairly foolish, but the result proves the importance of the spirit of our words. These children take their dog in their arms and say, "Oh, Boots, we think you're the most terrible dog in the world," but they say it with a soft, loving tone of voice. "You are so fat and ugly." And the dog starts licking their faces and wagging its tail and acting like it's in doggie heaven. But when the dog does something wrong, they will repeat the same insults, using the very same words, but in a harsh and scolding tone of voice, and the dog tucks in its tail and hangs its head in shame. The dog reacted totally to the tone of voice; the words meant nothing.

People, of course, understand the actual words; yet we too depend greatly on tone and inflection. If someone walks into your office and says, "Well, I see you are finally here!" the tone of the voice makes all the difference in the meaning of the words. The words can be warm and friendly, if the person has been looking forward to meeting you and has been waiting in the lobby. Or the words can be said harshly and sarcastically, if the person is an angry customer with a complaint to register. Many unnecessary misunderstanding arise over the tone of voice: "Well, the way you said that made me think," or "I didn't mean it the way it sounded."

As with our countenances, our words should not be manufactured sweetness. If we are established upon the rock of our salvation, our attitudes will be so rooted in God's ways and thoughts that gradually His character will become second nature, and finally first nature to us; then the reflections on our faces and the words and tones of our mouths will be genuinely godly. Some Christians do try to put on a pious show for people and it doesn't work. There is no fruit. Unless God builds the house, those who labor, labor in vain. If we try to construct our own structures, our own temples, it won't work. The winds will knock it down and we will be exposed as fakes. The world, with the sensitivity of the enemy, can spot a phony Christian a mile away. You can try to plaster a saintly look on your face and fake sweet words, but the inner man is still dark if the countenance and the words are not genuine. If you try, in your own efforts to manufacture the glory of God in your life, you will miss the great blessings of genuine love, peace, and joy.

God is calling us to consistency and maturity. One of the big problems with Christians is that we have different personalities we put on to suit the different places we go and people we meet. We have a Sunday-go-to-meeting personality; we have a family man personality; we have a work-week personality. We are not consistent and therefore the people who know and read us are confused. They do not see the glory of God all the time, so they're not sure what they are seeing. When we are at our best, and have our mirrors fixed upon God, the people at work don't know whether we are manifesting the glory of the Lord, or if we're just in a good mood because it's Friday. But if they see us at our best all the time, showing forth the glory of God all the time, they know it's God—it couldn't be anything else.

When my pastor is around, I can be the most spiritual man you can imagine. I have my mirror fixed on God. But at home or at work, when things don't go just right, I move my mirror. I reflect darkness and carnality. I may even speak religious words and smile religiously and do religious things, but I still reflect carnality. God wants consistency in our relationships with Him. He is leading us to consistency and demanding consistency in the critical age of the church. We are His Son's fiancee, and He wants for His Son a faithful and constant bride. If we are not faithful and constant, then we are not ready for His return, because He is coming for a bride without spot or blemish.

If you want to read your spiritual thermometer or EKG, don't measure only your church activities. Don't consider only your prayer time with your family. Don't count how many people you have witnessed to. These will not give you a complete reading of your spirituality. To measure your effectiveness, to find out really how spiritual you are, you must also ask yourself, "How do other people, the people at work, see me? What are they seeing in my mirror? What are they hearing in my words?" If people are not seeing the very image of God, then you are not very spiritual. Jesus can produce spirituality in you; He will appear in your countenance and your words, if you will but look to Him consistently in every aspect of your work.

CHAPTER FOURTEEN

Ordained Encounters

We have explored the importance of God's secret weapon, the living epistle, and also studied the power of words and countenance. The final aspect of our study on the Christian employee is that of personal encounters.

We often remark, "Hey, guess who I bumped into at the store?" To our way of thinking, we accidentally encountered someone; it was by chance that we saw each other. But when we studied the life of Joseph, we saw that none of Joseph's circumstances were merely situations of happenstance, but were intricately engineered by God. Now we must consider the truth that the people in Joseph's circumstances were also a part of that same intricate plan.

If we are to be effectively used by God, we must come to see that accidental encounters can, in reality, be ordained encounters, that God has a purpose when we bump into each other. God, knowing the heart of every man, knows precisely when that heart is prepared to receive a message from Him. Since He has already written that message on the tables of our hearts, He simply arranges a blind date so that the message can be delivered!

Just as God controls kingdoms and companies, regardless of their religious inclinations, so God is able to control individuals, regardless of their religious inclinations. If we are not aware of ordained encounters, we miss many opportunities to witness and share—and then wonder why God isn't using us more. An evangelist tells the story of a woman who wanted badly to witness, but she was home-bound during the day. He prayed with her for God to send to her door someone to whom she could witness, someone who needed to hear the gospel. A couple of days later, the woman spoke with the evangelist again, telling him of her disappointment—God had not sent anyone to her house, she said. The evangelist pressed further. "Not even one person came to your door that entire day?" he asked. The lady shook her head sadly, "No, no one came—except the Fuller Brush salesman." She realized at the moment that he was the one God had sent, but she had not been alert to this ordained encounter.

When we meet strangers or even familiar people, our natural reaction is: "If I say anything to him about Jesus, he is going to think that I'm a real fanatic"; or "What is this person going to think of me?" In other words, we are really saying, "I am more interested in my own reputation than I am in that person's eternal salvation." We are by nature totally self-centered. Jesus said that if we love another person, we will lay down our lives for them. So often, we would be willing to dive into water to save a drowning person, or jump in front of a truck to save the life of a child; but then we hesitate when it comes to opening our mouths to tell of God's love and grace. When we wonder what others are going to think of us, we are directing our attention, that is, our love, not to the person who needs God, but to ourselves.

When we bump into another person, our reaction should be, "What is God doing in this person's life? How can I help? Lord, show me why you have put this person in my path." At this point in our spiritual walk, we must become spiritual detectives. It is actually very exciting to play the part of a spiritual Sherlock Holmes. We can watch and listen for clues to tell us what God is doing in that person's life; and we can act on those clues. We should go through life viewing the people we meet as sent to us by God.

God made the truth of ordained encounters very real to me on an airplane trip to the West Coast some years ago. Normally, when I board an airplane, especially for non-stop flights such as this one, I immediately look for an aisle seat. I never enjoyed sitting in a window seat because I can't enjoy a meal cramped up next to the window; and I do not enjoy a middle seat because I inevitably end up between two 300-pounders. That day, however, when the man I was traveling with took the window seat, I chose the middle seat. I did not know what motivated me to do that at the time—but I do now.

In a few minutes, another man took the aisle seat beside me. He had a beard and wore blue jeans, but he was not shabby. He was clean and well-groomed. After the plane took off, my friend and I chatted for a while and I had occasion to open my briefcase to get some plans out. When I did, the young man beside me said, "Oh, are you an engineer?"

I answered yes and we began to talk. He had studied engineering in college and had made it to his senior year, when he had dropped out to go into business for himself with a chain of Laundromats. As we talked, the conversation came around to different philosophies of life. When our conversation took that turn, I fine-tuned my radar. I knew something was significant in our meeting. I began to pray, "Lord, tell me about this man. How do I touch him? What do you want me to do?"

Somehow the certain wording he used in talking about a particular subject provided me with the perfect opening to share with him what had happened in my life. I told him how empty I had been before I met God. I gave him my testimony in essence—and my testimony can get rather long. In fact, I testified from the Mississippi River to the Rocky Mountains. He was very, very attentive and he asked questions at various points in my story.

I arrived finally at the day I met the Lord. I told him that I had gone into the little church by myself early one morning and had knelt down and prayed, asking Jesus to come into my life. It seemed as though nothing happened and I got up to leave; but as I was walking out, I felt the Holy Spirit just invade my whole being. As I described this to him, he listened closely and I saw him shiver very slightly. I noticed it, but didn't think much of it and I continued to talk. About fifteen minutes later, I said, "Listen, would you like to know Jesus?" And he replied, "I already do. When you were telling me what you prayed that morning, I prayed it too." Then he said, "I felt Him come into me." That was the shiver I had seen, as Jesus had entered his heart.

That was one time I did not mind sitting in a middle seat. I do not know the young man's name, nor he mine. We were two total strangers meeting on an airplane, ordained by God to meet for a divine purpose.

In using these ordained encounters, we must learn to watch and listen for clues. We must learn to be alert to clues. We must be sensitive to the other person, watch his countenance and read his face. You don't have to be spiritually brilliant to read a person's countenance. If you walk into an office and the secretary is sitting at her desk with tears rolling down her cheeks, you know something is wrong. We should view problems—anyone's problems—as vehicles to take people toward God. When we see a problem, rather than shrinking away from it or from the person, we should try to find out how we can get involved in the problem and help that person. We should not walk up to a person and say, "I know that something is upsetting you and Jesus can help." We should not take that approach unless specifically lead by the Holy Spirit and I have found that He does not lead in that manner very often. Jesus got involved in the problem first, and then met the need. We are to use that same approach, demonstrating wisdom and compassion.

After you learn to read a countenance, listen carefully to the words a person speaks, listen carefully for verbal clues. People don't always say what they mean. It is difficult for a person to articulate what is going on inside, in the depths of his being, at any given moment. It's hard to put into words accurately what you are feeling, how you are hurting. If we are to be used in ordained encounters, we must learn how to listen. You might picture yourself putting your finger on a turning phonograph record to feel the knicks and scratches, for a broken place. From the words a person speaks, you can feel that place where that life has been hurt and wounded. As you feel these hurts, you pray, "Oh, yes, Lord, I feel it. This is where he has been hurt. What can I say to minister life, to heal the pain?" When Jesus stood in the synagogue to announce His mission, He read from the scroll of Isaiah that passage in which the prophet had prophesied of the coming Messiah. One of the reasons the Christ would come, according to this prophecy, was to heal the broken-hearted. God will give you directions to help heal that broken-hearted person you meet in an ordained encounter.

Where Will You Be?

There is a general unanimous feeling in the body of Christ all over the world that Jesus is coming back soon for His church. Christians all over the world have a sense of anticipation. In Matthew 24:14, Jesus said, "And this gospel of the kingdom shall be preached in all the world for a witness unto all nations; and then shall the end come." This is a promise and also a measuring stick for us. Before Jesus returns, the gospel will be preached to all the world. This is on the verge of becoming a reality today. Christian communications in the field of literature, radio and television as well as personal evangelism, are booming today. I have always looked upon this text, "the gospel shall be preached unto all the world," as meaning that Bibles and missionaries would finally reach to every corner of the globe. But now I see this verse in a new light. The preaching of the gospel of Christ is not dependent upon the distribution of Bibles. The Bible is made of paper and ink and leather, and the writtenWord will never be physically given to every person in the world. Spreading Bibles alone is not going to fulfill the requirement that the gospel shall be preached in all the world.

Likewise, it would be well nigh impossible to send enough missionaries to the countries of the world so that every person could hear a sermon and be offered an altar call. In America, we have churches on every street corner and the gospel communicated through the media virtually every hour of the day; yet this does not insure that the people of America hear the gospel preached. A very small percentage of Americans go to church. But the gospel will be preached all over the world in the form of the living epistle, known and read of all men. Individual Christians will preach the gospel in their homes and neighborhoods and communities all over the globe. That is the way, I believe, the gospel will be preached in all the world.

I can visualize enough living epistles scattered throughout the world, in every nation, so that every lost soul is in the process of reading the Word, the Christians, right now. Not everyone will believe, but everyone will have been preached to. They are being preached to by secretaries, department heads, government officials, and next-door neighbors. It is through Christian workers that the gospel will be preached in all the world. Employment has become crucially important. I can really picture the potential of all of us as living epistles, going every day to our offices all over the world, manifesting the Word of God to everyone. When everyone has read the Word of God in the living epistles, then I believe the trumpet will sound and the end will come.

When Jesus was instructing His disciples about His return, one asked Him, "Lord, when will it be?" Jesus answered him with these words: "Then shall two be in the field; the one shall be taken and the other left." Jesus will return on a work day. He will not come on a Sunday when everyone is sitting in church singing hymns, but when His followers are out in the fields working. The people who are His Body will be taken out of their places of employment, while they are sitting at their desks or working at their machines. They will be at the mill, at the factory, at the office, or on the airplane or in a board meeting. To me, it is an exciting idea that Jesus is not coming for a gathered church, but a dispersed church: one at that office, two from that department, five from that company. Jesus will come when His saints are at work, and being known and read by all men.

Jesus said to His disciples, "The harvest truly is

plenteous, but the labourers are few; Pray ye therefore the Lord of the harvest, that he will send forth labourers into his harvest" (Matt. 9:37-38). This is my prayer for you. And like Paul, I pray that God will establish you in every good word and work, so that when you stand before our Lord in that final day, you will hear these words:

"Well done, thou good and faithful servant."